RUSSIA

FLINT RIVER

RUS

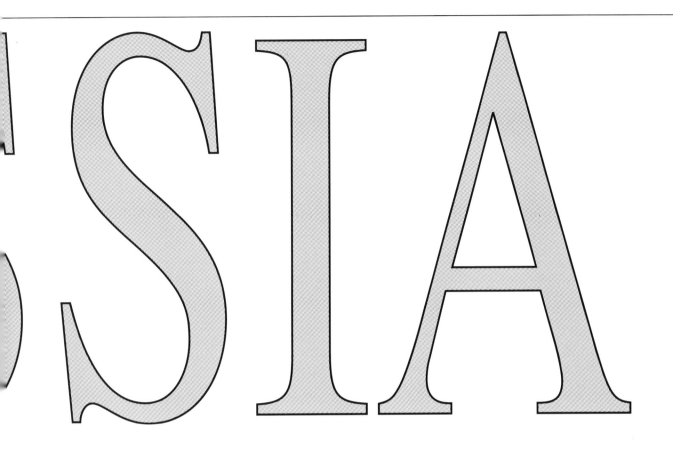

SSIA

Text and captions by

ROSANNA KELLY

A Motovun Group Book
© Flint River Press 1994

First published in the U.K. by
FLINT RIVER PRESS Ltd
143-149 Great Portland Street,
London W1N 5FB

2nd printing 1996

ISBN: 1 871489 16 4

Distributed in the Russian Federation by
Jupiter British Russian Joint Stock Co.,
Petrovka Street 8/11, Moscow 103031

Originated and developed by
Bato Tomasevic

Design
Gane Aleksic

Editor
Madge Phillips

Photographs:
Janusz Fogler: 43-64, 66, 68-71, 77, 78, 81-86, 90, 91
Victor Gritsyuk: 1-3, 6, 10, 11, 13, 15, 16, 18, 20-35, 37, 41, 75, 79, 80,
87-89, 92-94, 132-134, 145, 149, 150, 202-204, 206, 210, 212
Robert Harding Picture Library: 112, 126, 127
Paul Harris: 5, 17, 128, 165-170, 172-178, 182-188, 190-192, 194-196, 198, 200
Victor Korniushin: 7, 73, 102, 103, 129, 131, 135-140, 143, 144,
146-148, 151-162, 209, 211
Zbigniew Kosc: 65, 74, 76
Andrea Luppi: 96, 97, 106, 115-118, 120-125
Victor Poliakov: 19, 67, 95, 98-101, 104, 105, 107-111, 113, 114, 119, 141, 142
A. Rodionov: 8, 9
Mike Rutherford: 14, 38-40, 42, 199, 205
Victor Semionov: 4, 164, 171, 179-181, 189, 197, 207, 208
A. Volkov: 12, 36

The author is very grateful to George Lucas of the London School of Economics
for his invaluable advice on the economy,
and The Britain-Russia Centre for the use of their excellent library.

Typesetting by Avalon, London

Colour separation by Grafika Ilirska Bistrica, Slovenia

Organisation by Eurocity Associates Ltd, London

Printed in Slovenia byTiskarna Ljudska Pravica, Ljubljana

CONTENTS

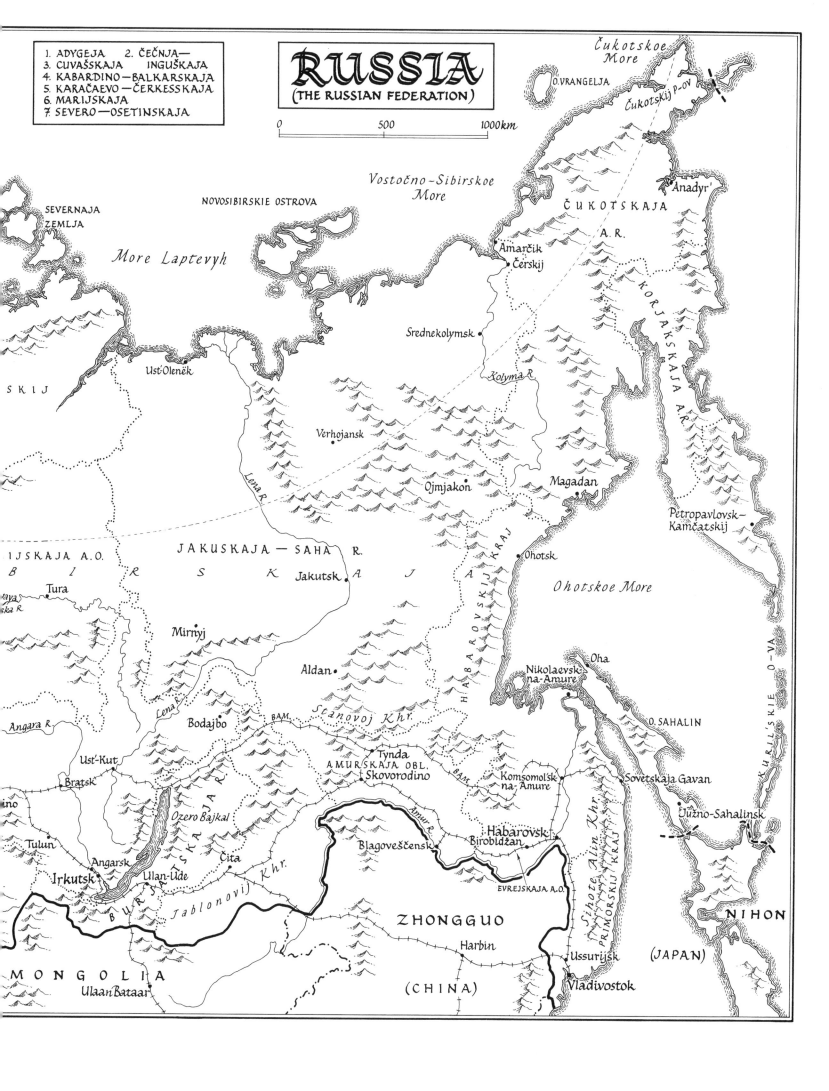

RUSSIA
(THE RUSSIAN FEDERATION)

1. ADYGEJA   2. ČEČNJA—
3. CUVAŠSKAJA   INGUŠKAJA
4. KABARDINO—BALKARSKAJA
5. KARAČAEVO—ČERKESSKAJA
6. MARIJSKAJA
7. SEVERO—OSETINSKAJA

0   500   1000km

Čukotskoe More

O. VRANGELJA

Čukotskij P-ov

Vostočno-Sibirskoe More

NOVOSIBIRSKIE OSTROVA

Anadyr'

ČUKOTSKAJA A.R.

SEVERNAJA ZEMLJA

More Laptevyh

Amarčik
Čerskij

SKIJ

Srednekolymsk

Ust'-Olenëk

KORJAKSKAJA A.R.

Kolyma R.

Verhojansk

Ojmjakon

Magadan

Petropavlovsk-Kamčatskij

IJSKAJA A.O.

JAKUSKAJA — SAHA   R.

Lena R.

Ohotsk

B   I   R   S   K

Tura

Jakutsk   A   J   A

Ohotskoe More

vaja)
ska R

Mirnyj

H
A
B
A
R
O
V
S
K
I
J
   KRAJ

Oha

Nikolaevsk-na-Amure

Angara R.

Aldan

Lena R.

Stanovoj Khr.

O. SAHALIN

Bodajbo

BAM

Ust'-Kut

Tynda
AMURSKAJA OBL.
Skovorodino

BAM

Komsomol'sk-na-Amure

Sovetskaja Gavan

KURIL'SKIE O-VA

Bratsk

Ozero Bajkal

Amur R.

Južno-Sahalinsk

Tulun

B
U
R
J
A
T
S
K
A
J
A
   R.

Čita

Blagoveščensk

Habarovsk
Birobidžan

Sihote Alin Khr.

PRIMORSKIJ KRAJ

Angarsk
Ulan-Ude

Jablonovij Khr.

EVREJSKAJA A.O.

Irkutsk

NIHON

MONGOLIA

ZHONGGUO

Harbin

Ussurijsk

(JAPAN)

Ulaan Bataar

(CHINA)

Vladivostok

FOREWORD

The Soviet Union has vanished, leaving scarcely a trace of its hammer and sickle behind. It had been founded in 1922 by the enforced union of Belorussia the Ukraine and the Transcaucasian Republic, with Russia. Eventually it consisted of 15 republics, ranging from the northern Baltic States to Georgia and Armenia in the south and eastward over Central Asia. Nearly seventy years afterwards, representatives of three of the four republics met in the Bialowieza Forest and signed a treaty marking the end of the Union. Ukraine, Russia and Belorussia (Belarus) are now independent countries, but are still linked through the Commonwealth of Independent States (CIS).

Russia, or the Russian Federation as it is known officially, is by far the largest state of the new Commonwealth, covering a total area of over 6.5 million square miles, spanning eleven time zones, and populated by 147 million people — over 80 per cent of them ethnic Russians. Stretching from the Baltic to the Pacific and encompassing within its territory immense differences in climate, economic conditions and cultural traditions, Russia is the largest administrative area in the world. Under Communist rule it was divided into 16 autonomous republics, five autonomous provinces, 10 national districts, six regions and 49 districts, a complicated structure that has been inherited by the Russian Federation of today.

For a millennium, the Russian state stood between East and West. Its roots were in the flourishing early medieval principality of Kievan Rus, which converted to Christianity in A.D. 988 and was strongly influenced by Byzantium. But its fate was to be invaded by the immeasurable Mongol-Tatar hordes, 'thick as a swarm of black arrows', who rode out of the Asian steppes. The Tatar invasion severed Russia from Europe from the thirteenth to the fifteenth centuries and left an indelible imprint. For the next five hundred years Russian history was one of territorial expansion. Like the North Americans, the Russians had a vast, sparsely populated continent at their disposal. Pioneer Russians migrated across Siberia, establishing the valuable fur trade and panning for gold and other minerals.

Russia's geography, past and culture are keys to understanding the complex problems faced by the country since the break-up of the Soviet Union at the end of 1991. In all its thousand-year history, Russia has never hitherto had a time of order without tyranny. As the nineteenth-century poet Polezhayev wrote: 'In Russia they worship the Tsar and the whip.' Yet the collapse of the Soviet Union was the result of Russia's move from repressive government by a Communist elite towards democracy. Regional differences and religion have been highlighted by recent events.

It is impossible to predict the future: how Russia will respond to the claims of its different peoples for greater independence, how it can change from Communism to capitalism, from dictatorship to democracy. Is its destiny to become, finally, an integral part of Europe? Has Russia really surrendered its imperial ambitions? The clues lie in its great past, its traditions and culture.

4. Wild, mountainous country forms much of southern Siberia, where spectacular Teletskoye Lake lies at an altitude of 1,430 ft amid the Altai and Sayan mountain ranges, to the west of Lake Baikal.

6. The nursery of Russian culture was the woodland (zaleskaya zemlya) of Central Russia, where the birch tree, almost a national symbol, reigns supreme (overleaf).

5. Kamchatka, the great peninsula in the Russian Far East on the Pacific Ocean is eleven time zones away from St Petersburg. A region with many volcanoes and huge forests, it is home to a number of ethnic minorities whose culture is akin to that of the native Americans.

7. Driving home at sunset: a sense of communion with Nature's varying moods and seasons is felt by many Russians, the majority of them not far removed from peasant roots. (pp.18-19)

8, 9. Shikotan, one of the most southerly of the Kuril Islands, which form stepping stones from Japan to the Kamchatka peninsula. The rock formations are volcanic, for the islands are part of the 'ring of fire' — the chain of volcanoes that encircles the Pacific. Under Russian administration since 1945, the islands are claimed by Japan.

10. The rocky peaks of the northern Caucasus (highest point Mount Elbrus, 18,585 ft), part of the snow-capped mountain belt stretching between the Black and Caspian Seas that forms a barrier between Europe and Asia.

*11. The Caucasus have been the subject of
legend since earliest times: here Jason
sought the Golden Fleece and Prometheus
was chained to Mount Kazbek (the second
highest peak) for giving the secret of fire to
mankind.*

AN INFINITY
OF SPACE

Unable to sleep on the night of 2 September 1913, Dr. Leonid Starokadomsky, who was exploring a sea route through the Arctic Ocean to the north of Russia, stood on the bridge of the Imperial Navy's ice-breaking steamer *Taimyr,* gazing at the ice floes, whilst in the chartroom, the ship's captain sat dozing, wrapped in an enormous sheepskin coat. As dawn was breaking, an unknown mountainous coast loomed through the haze on the horizon. It turned out to be an undiscovered archipelago — subsequently named the Severnaya Zemlya (Northern Lands) Islands. It was one of the last great geographical discoveries of the world, for so vast and inhospitable was Russia that even at the beginning of the twentieth century, some parts of the country had still not been explored.

'Oh, what a glittering, wondrous infinity of space the world knows nothing of! Russia!' wrote Nikolai Gogol in his celebrated novel *Dead Souls* in 1842.

The immensity of the Russian Federation is hard to imagine. Formed on 25 October 1917, it was the largest and most influential state to emerge from the break-up of the Soviet Union. With a total area of 6.5 million sq. mi., it is more than twice the size of the United States. Stretching across the Eurasian landmass to the Northern Pacific — the seas of Bering, Okotsk and Japan in the west and the Arctic Ocean in the north. It borders on the Black Sea and the Caspian Sea in the south, while its eastern boundaries lie along Kazakstan, Mongolia and China. At its furthest extent it clears 5,770 mi. from east to west, and 3,000 mi. from north to south. In consequence, most people live far from the sea, surrounded by the immense Russian plain, the largest stretch of lowland on earth.

Plains and Rivers

The poet, Mikhail Lermontov, wrote how he loved the landscapes of Russia: '...the cold silence of her plains, the swaying of her boundless forests, her flooded rivers, wide as the seas.'

Like mountains to Switzerland, so is the endless, low horizon to the greater part of Russia. Most of the land is open, empty and flat: in Russian legend the hero rides out across the open plain (average altitude of 650 ft), which spreads eastwards over more than two-thirds of European Russia and far into central Siberia. With few clearly-defined physical features to limit frontiers, Russians migrated outwards in search of virgin lands and maritime outlets.

Rivers have been the most important highways since remote antiquity. The North Dvina, the three mighty Siberian rivers: Ob, Lena and Yenisey, and the Amur all exceed 1,800 mi., ranking with the Nile, the Mississippi and the Amazon among the world's longest rivers. But the mother of all Russia's rivers is the Volga, described in a popular song as 'Russia's bitter tear, her wife and daughter'.

A major transport route from north to south and a source of hydro-electric energy, the Volga rises north of Moscow in the Valdai Hills, majestically flowing southwards for 2,190 mi., before breaking into one of the world's greatest river deltas on the Caspian Sea. Like the Nile, the Volga delta is flooded every spring, bringing life to the surrounding countryside — a designated area of natural beauty, although now gravely threatened by pollution from the industries and power plants upstream. Most astonishingly, the lagoons of the delta become a sea of pink flowers in summer, a floating carpet of hundreds and hundreds of lotus in full bloom, moving with the fluctuation of the delta itself.

12. The cone-shaped peak of Mount Vilyui in the southern volcanic range of Kamchatka. The peninsula has 160 volcanoes, of which 30 are active.

Mountains

Lermontov also admired the solemn glory of the wild Caucasus Mountains in the south:

> 'The flood of sunset; icy peaks between,
> Shining against the blue far off and dim,
> Such things alone had never changed for him.'

Like an impenetrable fortress, the Caucasus stand guard between Russia and Asia, their thousand jagged peaks stretching from the Sea of Azov to the Caspian Sea. The highest mountain in the Caucasus, in the Russian Federation and in the whole of Europe is Mount Elbrus (18,580 ft). Noah's ark was reputed to have passed through its twin peaks covered by eternal snows to reach Mount Ararat. The second giant of the Caucasus is Mount Kazbek (18,400 ft), to whose slopes, according to legend, Prometheus was chained by Zeus as punishment for giving mankind the gift of fire. Both mountains soar above Mont Blanc (15,770 ft).

By contrast to the Caucasus, the Urals, extending for more than 1,200 mi. from the Arctic Ocean to the steppes, and separating European Russia from Siberia, are modest in height, smoothed and worn away by wind and rain for over 300 million years. The highest peak, Mount Narodnaya, is a mere 6,217 ft. The Urals are famous for their valuable minerals and gemstones (rubies, emeralds, amethysts, sapphires). Many Russians living to the west of the Urals have never ventured across them. In 1957, a huge atomic explosion occurred in the southern Urals, where atomic waste had been stored for the previous ten years. The consequences were devastating: many people died, whole villages had to be evacuated, and some hundreds of miles were laid waste.

Beyond the Urals, the Yablonovy and Stanovy ranges, with peaks exceeding 6,562 ft, and the Sayan and Altai (over 10,000 ft) form a mountainous amphitheatre in south-east Siberia. Further east, smouldering volcanoes and spouting geysers characterize the landscape in Kamchatka. Mount Kluchevskaya (15,584 ft), the highest peak, is more than three times the height of Vesuvius and visible from 80 mi. away in clear conditions. It is one of the most active volcanoes in the world, having erupted over seventy times since records were begun in 1967. Further south, the comparatively low Sikhote Alin range in Ussuriland rises to an average 3,300 ft, completing the picture of Russia's highlands.

Seas and Lakes

The Caspian Sea, known to the Greeks as *Hyrcanium Mare* or *Caspium Mare*, is the largest inland sea in the world (total area 168,296 sq. mi.). Its wild shores were regarded as the home of savage beasts by Virgil, who mentions the 'Tigers of Hyrcania', and Shakespeare, whose Hamlet speaks of 'The rugged Pyrrhus like th'Hyrcanian beast'. But the Caspian has been tamed, like a dancing bear, into serving as a busy navigation channel between the Russian Federation and the Central Asian republics. Its waters are exploited for fishing, and its sea-bed for oil extraction.

About twelve million years ago, the Caspian was part of a larger body of water, connected to the Black Sea and the Sea of Azov, but it was left isolated by movements of the earth's crust which severed this link. However, the Black Sea (162,235 sq. mi.), always of great strategic importance to Russia as an outlet for its fleet, remained connected with the Mediterranean by the narrow gateway of the Bosphorus. The Sea of Azov, the shallowest sea in the world, with a maximum depth of only 46 ft, remained attached to the Black Sea by its umbilical cord: the Strait of

Kerch. The name of the Black Sea is thought to allude not to the dark colour of the waves, but to its stormy character, caused by the *bora*, a violent wind arising off the Caucasian coast. The Greeks, who were the seventh century B.C. colonizers of the Black Sea shores, called these unfriendly waters *pontos euxinos*, a euphemism for *pontos axinus*, meaning 'the inhospitable sea'.

Of the vast lakes dotted about the map of Russia, the three largest are Baikal (so big it is called the 'Northern Ocean') in south-eastern Siberia, and Ladoga (2,740 sq. mi.) and Onega (1,466 sq. mi.) in northern Russia. Baikal is the world's most ancient lake (25 million years old) and the deepest (5,751 ft). One fifth of the world's fresh water is contained within this enchanted lake with its inlets and shores fringed by massive mountains, great forests of fir trees and pockets of lush meadows. The purity of its water, maintained by a tiny crustacean that strains out bacteria and algae, is now gravely threatened by pollution from nearby factories and towns. The amount of polluted drainage tripled from 66 million cu. m. in 1986 to 192 million in 1988, making it likely that one more of the world's natural beauty spots will be destroyed by man.

Climate

Russia is one of the world's coldest and most northern countries, over half lying north of the latitude of 60 degrees, on the same level as Greenland and Alaska. It has a continental climate: long, freezing winters and short, hot summers with rainfall that is slight and ill-distributed — factors contributing to Russia's traditionally poor harvests. Winter lasts five months in St Petersburg (from November to March) but up to nine months in Siberia, with snow falling as late as May and frosts starting in August. Sub-zero winter temperatures are common in virtually the whole of the Russian Federation, but it gets colder further eastwards and northwards. The town of Oimyakon in north-east Siberia is the coldest inhabited place on earth, with temperatures recorded at more than 70 degrees C. below zero. Temperatures in the Far East can be almost as harsh as in the Siberian interior. Vladivostok, for example, despite its latitude and position on the sea, experiences average January temperatures of minus 14 degrees C., the result of the influence of strong, outflowing Siberian winds.

The sudden arrival of spring in Russia is announced by lighter frosts, by alternating snow and rain, by dampness everywhere. This is the *ottepel* or thaw. The ice breaks on the rivers, and the waters spill over the banks, inundating vast areas of land and making roads impassable. Winter garments are packed away and moths flutter out of wardrobes, before the onset of the heat, sunshine and thunderstorms of summer. Summer clothes the countryside in a beautiful profusion of wild flowers and great stretches of wheat and rye (although a third of the crop goes to waste because of the poor infrastructure). Motivated by a shortage of food in the shops, many people cultivate vegetables and fruits in their own kitchen gardens or at their weekend cottages (dachas). The growing season is so short and hot that the soil needs constant watering, weeding and other attention: a reason why summer is the busiest time of year for many Russians, in contrast to the long period of winter inactivity.

For two months in northern Russia by the Arctic Circle the sun never sets, but rolls along the horizon day and night. These long, northern evenings are known as the 'White Nights'. The brief Siberian summer is a time of burning heat, with temperatures reaching over 30 degrees C. in

Oimyakon, where they plummet in winter. The Far East of the Federation experiences monsoons in summer: from May to September the warm climate is tempered by the inflow of maritime air bringing monsoon rains.

Vegetation

Corresponding to climate and soil condition, there are six vegetation zones stretching across the country. From north to south, these are the tundra, taiga (or pine forest), mixed forest, steppe, semi-desert and desert. Each vegetation belt has distinct flora, fauna, wildlife and natural resources.

Patterned by thousands of lakes and rivers, the treeless tundra (a Finnish word for 'barren mountains') is the northernmost zone, sweeping across 3,000 mi., all the way from Finland to the Pacific Ocean. Permafrost below a layer of six in. makes farming virtually impossible, and only hardy plants such as lichen, moss, bilberries, whortleberries, cowberries and Arctic cotton grass can take root. In summer, the tundra's northern sea cliffs are the nesting ground of myriad kittiwakes, rosegulls, rock ptarmigans, guillemots and countless other migrating sea-birds. Most raucous is the Arctic parrot or common puffin. It nests, wrote an Arctic ornithologist, 'in crowds on rocky, tundra-covered islands, digging horizontal circular tunnels 50 - 70 cm. in length, at the end of which it lays an extraordinarily large and absolutely white egg'. The guillemots' pear-shaped egg is equally well designed for the narrow cliff shelves since it pivots without rolling off.

Having flown from their wintering grounds in the western U.S.A., about 60,000 snow geese find sanctuary every year in the nature reserve on Wrangel Isand in the Arctic Ocean, off the tip of north-eastern Siberia. They are observed by both Russian and American scientists, anxious to prevent them from becoming extinct. A polar bear surveying life from an ice floe, walruses crowding a beach, long-whiskered seals slipping off rocks into the sea, are among the sights of the tundra. Their future and the delicate eco-system of the tundra itself are threatened by dangerous radioactive elements that have spread over the Russian Arctic as a result of nuclear testing.

A Russian courier travelling by troika, nineteenth-century engraving.

The indigenous peoples of the north, such as the Evenks, Nentsi and Chukchi, have traditionally survived by reindeer farming (for meat, milk, hide and horns), driving their herds over hundreds of miles towards the northern shores, where tundra mosses and lichen provide summer pasture. Although industrial activity has expanded in the tundra, hunting and reindeer-breeding continue to be leading occupations. Fishing, whaling and seal-hunting are also organized on a large scale.

South of the tundra is the largest forest in the world, the taiga. In terms of timber resources, it is Russia's equivalent of the rain forest. Composed mainly of spruce and pine, the dark, forbidding forest covers a small part of north European Russia and most of Siberia, in all, an area of about 3 million sq. mi. In many parts it is impenetrable: a tangled web of thickets, impassable marshes, numerous lakes and swampy meadows. This is the habitat of mosquitoes and midges, frogs and toads, bees and ants, not to mention a great variety of bird and animal species, including an estimated 80,000 Russian brown bears, many living without the least risk of ever being glimpsed by man.

Human habitation of the taiga is made insufferable by the summer swarms of midges and mosquitoes, although sparse settlements are found along its river systems, having developed around ports, monasteries and trading posts. The villagers were traditionally hunters and gatherers rather than farmers: even where the forest is cleared for the cultivation of crops, the soil is usually poor and swampy. Instead, the taiga's wealth lies in its timber resources and furs: red and silver fox, squirrel, lynx, wolf, wolverine and, most highly prized of all, sable.

The taiga gives way to mixed coniferous-deciduous forest, which opens out towards the western border, joining up with the forests of central Europe. Lighter and more open than the taiga, the mixed forest has everywhere been partially cleared for farming. Further south, the trees thin out and the patches of grassland increase in extent. Here, in this wooded steppe, most of the land has been taken into cultivation. The true steppe, extending to the Caucasus and continuing as a broad band south and eastwards of the Urals and intermittently to Mongolia, is where grass alone dominates the landscape. But since the nineteenth century the better steppe has been cultivated for grain, which grows well in the fertile *chernozem.*

Zones of semi-desert and desert proper stretch south of the steppe, curling around the northern shore of the Caspian Sea, down to Azerbaijan. Traditionally, life in the semi-desert and desert regions was possible only at the water's edge, along the banks of rivers and rivulets, but artificial irrigation schemes have transformed the landscape. Where once pheasant and bustard built their nests and steppe antelope, deer and wild horses roamed, thousands of hectares of grain and rice are grown on the state farms with the help of fertilizers and pesticides.

Tundra, taiga and steppe; the mighty rivers majestically crossing the open plain; the extreme northern location, which makes a major part of the land unsuitable for farming: these are some of the general geographical features that have influenced the settlement, history and imagination of the peoples of Russia. Yet the main characteristic of the whole territory is its infinite space, a factor which doomed Russia to despotic rule, according to the eighteenth-century French philosopher Montesquieu, who believed that climate and geography determined the development of societies. And indeed, Russia has, historically, been held together by an authoritarian central government. The only exceptions to the prevailing centralism, to quote from the historian Richard Pipes, have been the result of 'administrative prudence and shortage of personnel'.

EUROPE AND ASIA

The Economy

Potentially one of the richest states in the world, Russia has a huge landmass with an abundance of raw materials and energy resources. It was by far the most populous state of the former U.S.S.R. and also much the wealthiest, producing 78 per cent of all its natural gas, 60 per cent of steel, 80 per cent of timber and 91 per cent of oil. It is, indeed, one of the world's foremost producers of these commodities (although it is now beginning to run out of easily exploited forests); it also has one of the world's largest fishing industries.

Productivity in all sectors of the economy is low, and throughout the country much produce is wasted because of poor organization and infrastructure, especially communications. Before the Revolution one of the world's largest grain producers and exporters, Russia became one of its biggest importers as a result of collectivization and mismanagement of agriculture. There were, and are, other hindrances. The climate over much of the country is one of extremes and much of the land is permanently frozen tundra or inaccessible forest. Nonetheless, large areas of the Federation can be used for agriculture. In 1991, grain and potatoes were the crops most widely grown. The poor grain harvest in 1991 and a collapse in food supplies forced the president to order the accelerated distribution of land to private farmers to boost production. Yet the agricultural reforms met with psychological resistance from many, accustomed as they were to state direction on land which was supposed to belong to everybody, but effectively belonged to nobody. Running deep in their psychology was a preference that all should be poor together, rather than allow the more enterprising to be better off.

This mind-set was not exclusive to farmers. Russian industry, too, remains bedevilled by a fear of change after seventy years of rigid state management. Its history goes back to the middle of the seventeenth century, when foreigners were granted rights to start glass manufacture. The development of new industries and crafts, notably metal working, textiles, brick making and china manufacture, was encouraged under Peter the Great. During the reign of Catherine the Great, the Urals became the focus for the iron industry and Russia ultimately became the world's largest iron producer. After 1870 a sharp rise in foreign investment stimulated an industrial boom, with railway engineering especially prominent. Some deals were made with western companies to develop Russia's immense oil resources. As a result oil production rose quickly and by 1903 Russia was the world's biggest producer, largely from fields in the Caucasus. Western companies also investigated the possibilities of natural gas reserves, which are among the largest in the world. By 1913 coal mining had begun in Western Siberia and in the Far East.

Pursuing their Marxist obsession with planned industry as the road to prosperity, the Communist Party forced the pace of industrialization. Millions of Soviet workers, poorly paid, badly housed, but enjoying a considerable measure of job security, joined in the efforts to catch up with and overtake the capitalist countries of the West. But the industrial sector built in the Communist era suffered from vital structural weaknesses. The central planning system was inefficient and wasteful as regards both production and distribution, while the labour force lacked incentives to work harder. Soviet manufactured goods became notorious for poor quality, but since trade was mostly with the members of Comecon, the economic organization of the Eastern bloc states, and there was a vast and hungry home market, there was little stimulus to improve quality or adopt new production and design methods.

By the 1980s the quality gap between home and western products could no longer be ignored, and calls for reform, always present, became widespread. Until its industry can be modernized, Russia will remain dependent on the energy sector. But output levels must be sustained. Oil production was 393 million tons in 1992, a fall of 15 per cent from 1991, and of 24 per cent from 1990. Production of natural gas, the other great energy resource, remained constant at around 640 billion cubic metres. Before 1986 it had been hoped that an expanded nuclear programme would aid the conservation of other energy resources, but after the Chernobyl disaster of that year, the plans were sharply curtailed. However, disposal of nuclear waste and the closing down of old nuclear power plants remain major problems of concern far beyond Russia's borders.

The Far North

What is now called the Far Northern Economic Region was once a remote place of exile, like Siberia, though nowadays foreign visitors go there to fish in its great rivers. Stretching over a vast area of 6,500 sq. mi., from Finland to the Urals and along the shores of the Arctic Ocean, it is the most sparsely populated area of European Russia. Bleak, treeless tundra by the coast gives way further south to forests and marshy swamps. Oil, gas, coal and timber resources, and the fishing industry make the region economically important. Prior to Russian expansion and colonization, it was inhabited by Finno-Ugrian tribes (the Karelians and Komi). By the fifteenth century many Russians had settled along the great ribbon-like north-flowing rivers. Two early saints, Savva and Zossima, founded the remote Solovetsky Monastery on the White Sea coast in 1346.

Until the fifteenth century, the main trading town of the Far North was Novgorod the Great on the River Volkhov, founded by the Ilmen Slavs over eleven centuries ago and one of the oldest towns in Russia. It developed extensive links with the Hanseatic League, trading with many western nations and using a German monetary system. Its territory and dependencies, extending far to the north and east, were criss-crossed with trade routes, linking up the towns it founded. Unlike the other medieval Russian states, Novgorod was a republic, governed by an assembly of citizens, though it also had a grand prince. But after its capture by Ivan the Great in 1478, Novgorod lost its independence to Muscovy and its prosperity steadily declined. The picturesque town now attracts tourists with its historical monuments and churches decorated with early frescoes. Sadko the Minstrel, Novgorod's shrewdest merchant, who is said to have made a deal with Neptune and used the profits to build a cathedral in the town, is the hero of local mercantile folklore.

St Petersburg, founded at the command of Peter the Great on the marshy shores of the Gulf of Finland in 1703, is the dominating city of the Far North and the second largest city of the Russian Federation, with a population of over four million. Variously called Petersburg, Petrograd and Leningrad, it became St Petersburg once again in September 1991. 'Other Russian cities are a wooden heap of hovels,' wrote Andrei Bely in *St Petersburg*, his early-twentieth-century masterpiece, 'but strikingly different from them all is St Petersburg.' Formerly the capital of the Russian Empire, the city is a major river and sea port and railway terminal. A multitude of industries — car-making, ship-building, chemical, paper and plastics — have accumulated along the river banks, contrasting with the stately palaces, huge squares and golden spires that transfigure the centre. With its magnificent architecture, its museums crammed with art treasures, and its

13. A rural childhood in the village of Nozhkino in Central Russia, north-east of Moscow. But village life holds little for young people: the infrastructure is undeveloped, public amenities and job prospects are poor, entertainment is lacking.

romantic White Nights, the city attracts many tourists.

To the north of St Petersburg, Petrozavodsk (pop. 270,000) on the shores of Lake Ladoga is the administrative centre of the Autonomous Republic of Karelia, mainly flat and forested, and dotted with over 40,000 lakes. Its Karelian inhabitants are closely related to the Finns.

An important sector of the region's economy is the timber industry, developed with aid from nearby Finland, though Karelian birch has long been used for furniture and decorative boxes. The fast north-flowing rivers (of which the greatest is the North Dvina) are ideal for floating timber. Many of Karelia's far-flung villages have beautiful wooden churches and ancient log cabins, examples of which have been transported from their original sites to be displayed at the open-air museum on Kizhi Island in Lake Onega.

Another local resource is high-quality stone, especially granite, marble and porphyry. The upper part of the Lenin Mausoleum on Red Square in Moscow and Napoleon's tomb in Paris are among the notable buildings faced with Karelian stone. The famous ballads of the *Kalevala*, the Karelo-Finnish national epic, were recorded in the area west of Kizhi and Lake Onega.

To the north-east lies the Autonomous Komi Republic, named after the Komi people, founded in 1936, an enormous, sparsely populated area with an economy based on gas and oil extraction and mining. The bare, northern tundra plains have an exceptionally severe climate and are covered by a blanket of snow for most of the year. Because of lack of roads, river transport is important, especially along the two largest rivers, the Pechora and Vychegda. The administrative centre, Syktyvkar, a place of exile in the nineteenth century, stands at the junction of rail and road routes. Of Komi's population of 1.3 million, only 290,000 are of indigenous stock, and even fewer speak the Komi language, which since 1990 has been promoted as the language of the republic.

Central Economic Region

14. An elaborately decorated wooden house, close to the ancient town of Vologda in northern Russia (overleaf). Houses of this type are common in villages and on the outskirts of towns.

15. A picturesque village on the shore of Lake Seliger in the Tver region, north-west of Moscow. The water is obviously clean enough to wash dishes in! (pp.36, 37)

Moving southwards, we come to the Central Economic Region with its typical Russian landscape of birch trees and rolling plains. The region is intersected by three great rivers, the West Dvina, Dnieper and Volga, all rising in the Valdai Hills. First mentioned in 1147, when it was a remote, wooden fortress, Moscow became the 'ruling Tsaritsa of Holy Russia' in the fifteenth century under Ivan the Great, who rebuilt the Kremlin as a symbol of his power. But in the early eighteenth century, Moscow suffered a great blow to its pride when Peter the Great moved the capital to his new northern city, St Petersburg. In 1918, however, Lenin transferred the capital back to Moscow. With a population of over eight million people, Moscow is the focal point of the Central Economic Region, where 20 per cent of the entire industrial output of the former Soviet Union was concentrated.

Around Moscow there are many places of interest that can be visited on a day trip: the Troitse-Sergieva Lavra at Zagorsk, one of the oldest and most revered monasteries in Russia; Chekhov's house, now a museum, at Melikhova; near Tula (the 'Birmingham of Russia'), Tolstoy's estate, Yasnaya Polyana — a low white house set amid birch woods, meadows and lakes; the great palace and gardens of Arkhangelskoye, which once belonged to Prince Yusupov, said to have been even richer than the tsar. Also nearby is the battlefield of Borodino, where the French and Russian armies fought during the Napoleonic War.

16. On Kizhi Island, Lake Onega, examples
of traditional wooden dwellings have been
'collected' for an open-air museum of folk
architecture. Only a few of these spacious
log houses (izbas) remain, and the skills
needed to construct them are in danger of
dying out. Note the ramp for carts leading
to the working quarters on the upper floor.

17. Freshly caught from the river, the fish
are salted and then dried. In the right conditions, they will keep for as long as five
years. Farmers take such fish to the fields
for lunch with some rye bread and perhaps
an onion or carrot.

18. *A wooden windmill has been preserved for posterity at the open-air museum near the village of Yamka on Kizhi Island, Lake Onega. In the past almost every village would have had at least one, standing on an exposed site outside the settlement. Larger villages would have 30 or more. Now windmills have all but vanished from the countryside.*

*19. Birch trees beside water on the out-
skirts of the former fortress town of Ples in
the province of Ivanovo, founded in 1410 to
protect the eastern border of Muscovy.
Landscapes like this have inspired
innumerable Russian painters.*

20. Horses still have a role to play in farming, as here in the Tula region of Central Russia. The writer Lev Tolstoy lived most of his life in this province, at his country estate of Yasnaya Polyana. During his lifetime, the town of Tula was famous for its metalworking, manufacturing weapons and also samovars.

21. A track through the countryside near the village of Spasskoe-Lutovinovo, where the writer Ivan Turgenev had his estate, some three or four hours' drive from Moscow in the Orel region.

22. The main street of the ancient town of Galich, near Kostroma in Central Russia (overleaf). Smaller towns with their dirt roads and sparse traffic are scarcely more urbanized than large villages.

23. A farmer and his horse and cart
(telega) in the town of Nizhny Sergi in the
southern Ural Mountains. Though parts of
the mineral-rich central and southern
Urals have been heavily industrialized,
elsewhere the slow pace of rural life
remains unchanged.

24. The farmer is wearing standard winter garb for the countryside: fur hat (shapka), padded coat (fufaika) and felt boots (valenki). The horse's traditional curved and decorated wooden harness is known as a duga.

26. *A priest officiates at a graveside in a village not far from the Optina Puystyn Monastery in the Kaluga region, south of Moscow. Since the fall of Communism, religion has been practised more openly and widely, in a manner unthinkable under the former regime.*

25. *At Russian funerals, the coffin is customarily left open until just before burial so that family and friends can bid a last farewell. There is also the element of demonstrating publicly that the person is actually deceased.*

27. Seemingly untouched by the twentieth century, this rural scene is in fact on the outskirts of the small town of Ples, Ivanovo region, on the banks of the Volga between Kostroma and Nizhny Novgorod.

28. Wooden church in the village of Man'ga in Karelia, the forested region dotted with lakes that borders on Finland. Russians began settling in this region populated by Finno-Ugric tribes in the tenth century. By the mid-fifteenth century, most Karelian lands had been taken over by Novgorod boyars.

*29. The outskirts of Sergiev Posad
(Zagorsk) in the Moscow region. The range
of vehicles on the dusty road is typical, and
so are the kerchiefed women, interrupting
their chat to stare at the camera.*

30. *A forest of telephone poles not far from Lake Seliger, Central Russia. There are about 15 telephone lines for every 100 Russians, only a quarter the number in the USA, though the proportion in big cities is much higher. Since local calls are free, a lot of time is spent on the phone.*

31. Years of hard toil and harsh climate have etched the faces of these workers in a timber yard in the village of Gridino on the White Sea coast. The main city and port of the region is Arkhangelsk (Archangel), from which timber and other products of the Far North are exported.

32. *A dog's place in rural Russia is rarely in the home, but outdoors, chained near its kennel, so it can fulfil its purpose in life: to guard property. This thick-furred variety, akin to the husky, is tough enough to with-stand the cold of the Far North.*

33-35. Timber, the traditional Russian building material, continues to be used for housing and other structures in many parts of Russia. Some dwellings are carefully crafted and have fine carved decoration, others are rough-and-ready. In either case, wood is cheaper and warmer than stone. Even wooden sidewalks and pathways, common in cities until the beginning of the century, are still laid down in some places.

36. The troika ('threesome'), so called
because it is drawn by three horses,
is the most romantic way of travelling in
winter. The centre horse is always the most
powerful, while those on either side are
trained to bend their arched necks away
from him, to enhance the graceful beauty of
the team in motion. Small bells attached to
the harness tinkle as the troika races across
the snowbound countryside.

37. Travelling along the muddy roads during the spring thaw is less romantic, and
much slower. This is the village of Polkh
Maidan in the region of Nizhny Novgorod
(renamed Gorky in Soviet times), a city
once famed for its trade fairs. The difficulty
of getting there along such roads is
perhaps not much less nowadays than that
encountered by medieval merchants.

38. *This tractor-driver in the Nizhny Novgorod area is proud to own his farm.* Private farming has been encouraged since the late Eighties: in 1991 there were some 50,000 smallholdings in Russia. Though these are the main producers of potatoes and other vegetables, many people have reservations about private ownership of land. The tradition of villages holding land in common was widespread in northern and central Russia long before Communist collectivization.

39. *The face of a 'babushka' (opposite), who has toiled a lifetime on a state farm near Kursk.* In the close-knit Russian family, three generations often live together. The grandmother commonly survives her husband. According to the latest statistics, the average life expectancy for men has fallen in the past few years to 59 years, the lowest level since the 1960s, while women live on average 73 years.

40. *Tending goats by the roadside near Sergiev Posad (formerly Zagorsk). With food in short supply, peasants who own livestock and grow vegetables (she is sitting on a sackful of greens) find a ready market for their produce in nearby towns. Like many peasants the world over, she preferred not to have her face reproduced on a photograph.*

41. *A sunlit path through the forest in high summer, the season for expeditions into the countryside to pick berries and mushrooms. From earliest times the forests provided wax and honey, bark for shoes and parchment, and timber for building and fuel.*

West of Moscow, the largest industrial town is Smolensk, pleasantly situated on hills on either side of the River Dnieper and compared to Rome by the French writer Stendhal, who came to Russia with Napoleon's Grand Army. To the north and west of the capital, a string of medieval Russian towns with glistening golden domes, such as Rostov and Yaroslavl on the Volga, are great tourist attractions. South of Yaroslavl is the old town of Kostroma with its flax mills and engineering factories. From Kostroma it is not far to Ivanovo, another industrial town, and the nearby village of Palekh, renowned for its craftsmen working in lacquer and papier maché. East of Moscow lie Suzdal, Rostov and Vladimir, with their picturesque, typically Russian architecture and to the south, Oryol, with its feel of old provincial Russia and, not far away, the house of the writer Turgenev at Spasskoye Lutovinovo.

Nizhni-Novgorod (Gorky in the Soviet period), the third largest town in the Russian Federation with over a million inhabitants, is situated in the Volga-Don region, at the confluence of the Volga and the River Oka. It was called 'Nizhni' (Lower or Lowland) to distinguish it from Novgorod the Great in the Far North. With its namesake, it also shares a long mercantile tradition: before 1917 its annual fair was the largest and most famous in Russia.

During the Soviet period, Nizhni-Novgorod, with one of Russia's largest defence industries, was closed to foreigners; the dissident Andrei Sakharov was exiled there. By then its historic name had been changed to Gorky, in honour of the revolutionary writer Maxim Gorky, a native of the town. But though he was favoured by the regime, Gorky's descriptions of life in Russia's heartland were not entirely complimentary. Visiting the nearby town of Arzamas (the second largest city in the Nizhni-Novgorod district) he wrote in his diary: 'I do not think there is any other country where people talk such a lot and think so incoherently ...as they do in Russia, particularly in provincial Russia.'

European South-East

42. Geese, raised for food and feathers, have always been a part of Russian rural life and often feature in fairy tales and folk-lore. A peasant woman keeps an eye on her small flock in a village in the foothills of the Caucasus Mountains.

South of Nizhni-Novgorod lie the rural lands along the banks of the Volga that were the domains of Turkic and Finnic peoples who came under Russian rule in the sixteenth century. The autonomous republics in this region bear the names of the six main non-Russian peoples: the Turkic-speaking Tatars, Bashkirs and Chuvash, and the Finno-Ugrian-speaking Mari, Mordvins and Udmurts. All of them have been in close contact with the Russians for centuries. They are, in fact, physically indistinguishable when winter arrives in rural areas and foresters and farmers, Russians and non-Russians alike, don an identical costume of hat (*shapka*), thick, grey, padded coat (*fufaika*) and warm, felt boots (*valenki*) as essential protection against the cold.

The non-Russian peoples of the Volga basin are, over all, outnumbered by ethnic Russians, though the Chuvash make up 67 per cent of the population of Chuvashia and the Udmurts half the population of Udmurtia. The Kazan Tatars, however, comprise only 47 per cent of the population of Tatarstan (mixing with Russians, Chuvash, Maris, Udmurts, Jews, Ukrainians, Bashkirs and others). The Bashkirs, the Maris and the Mordvins are minorities in their respective autonomous republics. Nevertheless, since the collapse of the Soviet Union, two of the Volga autonomous republics with large Muslim populations, Tatarstan and Bashkortostan, have sought greater independence from Moscow.

Udmurtia, the northernmost autonomous republic of the Volga region, situated on the gentle western slopes of the Urals in the Kama river basin, takes its name from the Finnic Udmurts (or Votyaks as they were called until 1932). The greater part of Udmurtia is covered by coniferous forests, though wheat and other cereals are cultivated on large areas of farmland. The economy, however, is not entirely agriculture-based, as demonstrated by the industries in the administrative centre, Izhevsk, which boasts the first motor-cycle factory to be built in the former Soviet Union, and a large gas-generating plant. Udmurtia's second largest town, Votkinsk, developed into an important metallurgy centre making trains and rolling stock for the Siberian railways. It was the birthplace of the famous composer Peter Tchaikovsky, whose engineer father managed the Votkinsk Department of Mines from 1840 to 1848.

The Mari Autonomous Republic lies between the Volga and the Viatka rivers to the south-west of Udmurtia. Most of it stretches along the Volga's flat and heavily wooded banks, and its chief wealth consists of timber — spruce and silver fir. The republic's administrative centre, Yoshkar-Ola, founded as a Russian frontier post in the sixteenth century, has grown from a village of about 2,000 before the Revolution to a town of over 300,000 inhabitants, many employed in the timber mills and agricultural machine works. The indigenous Mari people, some 600,000 in number, have a history of long contact with the Turkic Tatars and Bashkirs, though they themselves are of Finnic origin. Sometimes known as the Cheremissi or Tcheremissi, they formerly led a pastoral life, but, to quote a young Englishman, Robert Johnston, who travelled around Russia, albeit in 1814, they 'have since imitated their Russian conquerors and cultivate the land'.

South of Mari lies Chuvashia, home of the Chuvash, descendants of the Turkic-speaking Bulgars who ruled over the southern part of European Russia during the tenth and eleventh centuries. (A branch of these moved to the Balkans and settled on the territory that is now Bulgaria.) The Chuvash are the only non-Finnic people of the upper Volga, although their language is strongly influenced by the Finno-Ugrian tongues of their neighbours. They traditionally inhabited the densely forested, hilly territory between the rivers Sura and Sviayag, two of the Volga's tributaries. Chuvashia's forests, famous for the Chuvash oak, are exploited by the timber industry, an important sector of the republic's economy. The capital, Cheboksary, a major junction for the Moscow-Siberian railway, is a modern, industrial town situated on a hill overlooking the Volga where a vast reservoir has been created.

Moving south-westwards to the black-earth forest steppe between the rivers Moksha (a tributary of the Oka) and Sura, we come to the Autonomous Republic of Mordvinia. The Finnic Mordvins, about 340,000 in number, consist of two branches, the Erzya and the Moksha, whose dialects differ so greatly that they may be considered separate languages. Mordvinia's administrative centre, Saransk, has considerable light industry: engineering, electrical equipment and tobacco, and supplies light bulbs to the whole region. The town is distinguished by a museum of the work of the Mordvinian sculptor S. D. Erzya, and also an art gallery with works by well-known Russian painters, established as a result of the Soviet policy of bringing Russian culture to the provinces.

Oil-rich Tatarstan lies to the east of Mordvinia, across the Volga. Its ancient capital, Kazan, where Tolstoy and Lenin went to university, and the world-famous bass, Fedor Chaliapin, was born (1873), was founded in the thirteenth century by the Kazan Tatars, a Turkic people who had adopted Islam by the tenth century and controlled a flourishing empire (khanate).

But in 1552 Kazan was captured by Ivan the Terrible and the Mongol (i.e. Tatar) Kazan khanate was destroyed. The only Muslim monument built of stone to survive the Russian invasion was the Suyumbika Tower, which now stands among the Orthodox Christian churches in the Kazan kremlin (citadel). During the Revolution, White Russian forces made Kazan their stronghold. After their defeat, the Tatar Autonomous Republic was founded by the victorious Bolshevik government in 1920. For the next seventy years of Communist rule, the learning of the Tatar language was discouraged, as was the practice of the Muslim faith. After the collapse of the Soviet Union, Tatarstan declared its sovereignty in August 1991. This declaration was accompanied by a revival of religious, social and political life, and growing support for the view that the natural wealth of Tatarstan, its oil reserves and considerable industrial output, should belong to the republic itself.

Besides the Tatars living in the autonomous republic and elsewhere in the Volga and Urals regions, who are more European in type, there are the Astrakhan and Siberian Tatars, who are closer to the Mongols in appearance. The Tatars of the Crimea, granted their own autonomous republic in 1921, were deported *en masse* to Central Asia in 1944 for collaboration with the Germans. Some of these have now returned. Most Tatars are Sunni Muslims, though there is an Orthodox minority in Tatarstan.

Neighbouring Bashkortostan (Bashkiria), the oldest of the Russian Federation's autonomous republics, dating from 1919, has also demanded greater independence. But the Muslim Bashkirs, a Turkic people closely related to the Tatars, make up only 38 per cent of the population: the rest are Russians, Tatars, Chuvash and others. Their demands are unlikely to meet with the approval of Moscow, especially since Bashkortostan has rich oil fields in the Urals, as well as reserves of natural gas, timber, coal, salt and numerous ores. Iron and copper mining in the Ural Mountains and

Tatars returning to the University of Kazan, nineteenth century

Bashkortostan began in the eighteenth century as the result of the efforts of Peter the Great to equip his armies in the Great Northern War against Sweden. The capital of the republic, Ufa, with over a million inhabitants, is in the heart of Bashkortostan, on the right bank of the River Belaya, just below the point where it is joined by the River Ufa. A centre of industry and a major junction of railways, roads and oil and gas pipelines, the city and its river have suffered accordingly. Its modern face was described by Simon Vickers, the first Briton to cross the former Soviet Union by bicycle, in 1990: 'We cycled to the centre, hoping to find some redeeming architecture, something to look at, an old quarter perhaps. But we found nothing. We bounced over railway tracks, past heaps of metal and concrete, archaic-looking factories with broken windows, rusting metalwork and leaning fences. Black clouds streamed from blackened chimney-pots of brick; yellow buses, their windows blotted out with dust and grime, lurched over the tramlines, where queues of people waited patiently, poker-faced.'

No description of Bashkortostan would be complete without mention of the sturdy Bashkirian breed of horses and of *kumys*, the drink made of soured and fermented mare's milk for which the country is famous. There is a story of how the writer Lev Tolstoy travelled to Bashkiria in the early 1860s in order to drink *kumys*, renowned for its medicinal qualities, and breathe the fresh air of the steppe.

West of Ufa, leaving behind the forests, marshes and bogs of the autonomous republics, the Volga flows indifferently southwards to the drier, treeless, prairie plains and salt marshes of its lower reaches. Several major towns are passed on the way: Ulyanovsk (formerly called Simbirsk), the birthplace of Lenin; Samara (formerly Kuibyshev), which became virtually the capital of the U.S.S.R. during the Second World War, when German troops were advancing on Moscow; and then Saratov, with all its streets running down to the Volga at its feet.

On Baedeker maps from the turn of the century, many of the villages north of Saratov have German and Swiss names, for long ago Catherine the Great settled Germans with some Ukrainians and some Estonians on the banks of the Volga. After the Revolution, in 1924, the German Autonomous Republic was created along the southern Volga, but it was abolished in 1941, when the ethnic Germans were mostly deported to Kazakstan for anti-Soviet activities. In 1988 an estimated two million ethnic Germans moved to Germany from Russia, bringing with them what little they could.

From Saratov, the Volga heads towards the great steppes, flowing indolently but inexorably between desert lands, past soft grey banks with only a narrow fringe of reeds and aspens. The boat trip to the next major river port of Volgograd (formerly Stalingrad and before that Tsaritsyn) takes thirty-six hours. Eventually, great factories, grain elevators and oil tanks loom into view, spreading for almost fifty miles along the river banks. Volgograd (then Stalingrad) was the site of one of the fiercest and biggest battles of the Second World War, when the city was devastated.

The last port of call is Astrakhan, lying on an island entwined in the arms of the Volga and its tributary, the Bolda. The lovely old town is dominated by its white, sixteenth-century kremlin with a Baroque cathedral, standing on a small hill and surrounded by traditional wooden houses. Astrakhan is in the very heart of the drowsy Russian south, with all its associations of melons and caviar. But it is also one of Russia's most important ports on the Caspian Sea and a southern outlet for Russian commerce.

The country to the west of the city on the shores of the Caspian Sea became the Autonomous Republic of Kalmykia in 1935. A sparsely populated, mainly desert and semi-desert land, its capital is Elista (meaning 'sandy'). The Kalmyks (or Kalmuks), who make up 80 per cent of the population, are a Buddhist, Mongol people, who migrated westwards from the western Siberian steppes in the late seventeenth century.

They were meticulously described by Professor Pallas, a German professor invited to Russia by Catherine the Great, as being 'in general of a moderate stature, well-made, but thin; their faces are remarkably flat, particularly their noses; their eyes are small and narrow, with the corners towards their temples pointing downwards; their lips are thick, their hair black, their complexions tawny, and their ears remarkably large, and standing wide from their head... In consequence of riding so much on horseback and their mode of sitting cross-legged, the Kalmuks are generally bow-kneed.' The Kalmyks were deported by the Stalinist state to Siberia after the Second World War and only rehabilitated in 1957.

The North Caucasus

The North Caucasus is a geographical term used to describe the steppes to the south of Kalmykia and the northern slopes of the Caucasus Mountains themselves. Some of Russia's greatest writers, as well as native poets, have been inspired by the solemn glory of the mountains, the legends and customs of the wild, free highlanders, mounted and bearing arms, and the more colourful episodes of North Caucasian history. The fabled peaks of Elbrus and Kazbek; the 'blood-snows' caused by oxides of iron-bearing rock tingeing the glaciers; the River Terek, a name famous throughout Russia in the nineteenth century as the frontier with the highlanders of the Caucasus; the mountain streams — all these have been described by some of the most celebrated Russian and foreign writers, among them, Alexandre Dumas.

The magnificent mountain barrier, long considered of vital strategic importance by the tsars, since it separated the Russian and Ottoman empires, was only conquered in the second half of the nineteenth century after the most protracted and fiercest campaign of Russia's history. Another struggle was needed in the early 1920s before the Bolsheviks managed to incorporate the North Caucasus into the newly formed Russian Federation. Even now the Caucasian nations have not given up their fight for independence: since the collapse of the Soviet Union, a number have demanded freedom from Moscow and the creation of a Federation of the Mountain Peoples of the Caucasus, away from the Russian sphere of influence.

The presence of Islam is widespread in the North Caucasus, and nowhere more than in the solidly Muslim Autonomous Republic of Daghestan (a Turkic word meaning 'Land of the Mountains'), which occupies the eastern end of the Caucasus and the land descending from the rugged mountains to the western shore of the Caspian Sea, where oil is refined in the port of Makhachkala, the capital of the republic. The Muslim mountaineers of Daghestan were among the fiercest fighters in the Holy War or *Ghazawat* against the Russian 'infidels' during the nineteenth century. They were led by the warrior-prophet Imam Shamyl, who was born in the mountain village of Ghimri in north-eastern Daghestan. During the almost thirty-year-long Holy War of resistance, Shamyl's fame spread from Daghestan west into Chechnia, where the Chechen highlanders rallied to fight with him in defence of their faith and freedom. After years of successful guerrilla warfare, which engaged large Russian military resources, in 1859 Shamyl was finally taken prisoner and the Caucasian war officially ended. However, the memory of the long fight remained vividly alive among the Chechens and Daghestanis, who, while accommodating themselves to Russian rule, never became fully reconciled to it.

At least nine different languages are spoken officially and numerous others are in use in Daghestan (the Arabs call it the 'Mountain of Tongues'). A Muslim legend explains that as Allah's envoy was galloping across the earth distributing languages to people, his way was barred by mountains. When his horse stumbled on a steep path, the messenger dropped his saddlebag, scattering the languages. Another explanation is that in the course of history different peoples passing through Daghestan became lost in the deep valleys and pathless mountains, and settled down in linguistic isolation. There are three main ethno-linguistic groups: the Turkic, in the steppes of the northern foothills and in the extreme south; the Persian (Iranian), established on the coast between Derbend and Baku; and the Ibero-Caucasian group, living in the middle and high mountain ranges.

The small, inaccessible Chechen and Ingush republics (until recently united) in the mountains, foothills and plain zone to the west of Daghestan, were noted primarily for their agriculture and particularly livestock breeding and for oil refining and chemical industries around the city of Grozny. The Chechens, who belong to the Caucasian language group, have a reputation as rebels and for the immense significance they attach to the Muslim faith. Traditionally, their communities were made up of large families and clans, whose members considered themselves equal and abided by a strict code of honour and spirit of chivalry. The Ingush, like the Chechens, belong to the Caucasian family group and are Muslim. Their code of honour was equally strict. According to John Baddeley, a traveller to the Caucasus in the nineteenth century, '...an Ingush girl won't marry her lover until he has killed five men and stolen one hundred sheep or the equivalent.'

The nominally Christian Ossetians of North Ossetia found it easier to adapt to western practices than their Muslim neighbours. The Ossetians are descended from the Alans, who lived in the plains between the Don and the Caspian in the early centuries A.D. and built up a powerful state that had links with Rome and Byzantium in the seventh and eighth centuries.

Tatar village near Kazan, in the nineteenth century.

Overwhelmed by Mongol forces in the twelfth century, they were pushed back into the high mountain ranges. North Ossetia was incorporated into the Russian Empire in 1774. Its capital, Vladikavkaz, (in Soviet times Ordzhonikidze) stands on the banks of the foaming River Terek, where the river leaves the mountains and rushes through the town in a rocky valley.

Overlooked by the austere foothills of Mount Kazbek (the peak is in nearby Georgia), the town is at the start of the famous Georgian Military Highway, connecting the North Caucasus to Georgia. The highway runs along the deep and narrow Daryal ravine and zigzags up to the Krestovy Pass (7,805 ft), named after a stone cross on the summit of Mount Krestovaya. From the top of this pass, much higher than any in the Alps, the road descends into Georgia. The route has been known from time immemorial and the Daryal Gorge, through which it enters the main range of the Great Caucasus, was the Caucasian Gates, mentioned by Pliny, that marked the limits of the domains of ancient Rome. After the unification of Georgia and Russia in 1801, the Russian Military Administration was charged with the building of a more reliable road. By 1817 the whole length had been opened to the public. Besides the spectacular Georgian Military Highway, other remarkable man-made features in North Ossetia are the tall dwelling-towers, burial-towers and watch-towers, some dating back to the days of the Mongol invasion, in the scattered highland villages.

The Autonomous Republic of Karbardino-Balkaria, west of North Ossetia, is a land of fertile fields, orchards and good pasturage on the mountain slopes, and also noted for its deposits of molybdenum (used in alloying steel) and tungsten mined in the mountains, which occupy almost half the republic's territory. The capital, Nalchik, founded as a Russian fortress in the nineteenth century, lies in the foothills beside the mountain river of the same name. The republic's population is made up of Karbardins, a Caucasian people, Balkars, who are Turkic-speaking, and Russians. The Christian Karbardins, renowned for their skilled horsemanship, svelte and noble figures, and handsome aquiline noses, occupied the strategic central sector of the Northern Caucasus, which enabled them to gain control over the entire North Caucasian plain and dominate most of the other native highlanders. Traditionally, they have grown grain and bred horses and cattle. The Balkars, on the other hand, have mainly engaged in making woollen cloth and felt rugs and in metal working.

The Urals

From time immemorial, the Ural Mountains have been regarded as the border between Europe and Asia. To the west of the Urals lies European Russia, the cradle of Russian culture; to the east, 'the slumbering land' of Siberia, its very name carrying connotations of icy wastes and political repression. The Ural Economic Region is one of the most industrialized in the Russian Federation, partly due to the fact that many factories making arms and other essentials were moved there during the Second World War when western parts of the country were invaded. The legendary mineral wealth of the Urals includes rich deposits of iron, copper, bauxite, titanium, chromite and platinum, as well as nickel, lead, zinc, silver, gold, cobalt, tungsten, malachite, marble, asbestos, and many kinds of gems.

The mountains, in general, lack the grandeur of the Caucasus, but the valleys are picturesque, their wooded slopes clothed in fir, pine, spruce, and some oak and linden. In the far north, tundra vegetation prevails. The higher peaks are in the north: Mount Narodnaya, the loftiest, reaches 6,217 ft. Large areas of the north and centre are still virgin forest, with deep lakes, mountain streams and waterfalls. In the central part of the Urals, where most of the industry and the biggest towns, such as Yekaterinburg, are concentrated, the mountains are generally lower and offer a gateway from European Russia into Siberia, the roads and railways following the deep-cut valleys. The great highway into the Urals from the south and west is the River Kama, which was part of the ancient overland trade route from India via the Caspian Sea and the Volga to the North Dvina River and Archangel.

The Slumbering Land

Asian Russia is divided into three geo-economic regions: Western Siberia, Eastern Siberia, and the Far East, with the rivers Yenisey and Lena taken as the demarcation lines. This huge area has immense mineral and other natural resources, but the great distances, lack of infrastructure and harsh climatic conditions make much of this potential wealth difficult and expensive to exploit.

Siberia, the mythical, wild land beyond the Urals, is almost the size of Europe and larger than the U.S.A. It extends for 4,350 mi. from the Urals in the west to the Pacific Ocean in the east, and for over 2,000 mi. from north to south, from the Arctic Ocean to China and Mongolia. Many of the settlements are linked to the outside world by only the roughest tracks. The best way to travel locally is along the waterways: by sledge in winter, when the rivers are covered by ice up to ten feet thick, and by canoe in summer. The main overland communications line is, of course, the Trans-Siberian Railway.

The origin of the word Siberia is disputed. It may derive from the Mongolian word *siber* meaning 'pure' or 'beautiful', or it may mean 'slumbering land', from the language of a nomadic tribe. For who knows what reasons, many thousands of years ago numerous tribes trekked northwards from the warm plains of Central Asia to Siberia's tangled forest depths and desolate tundra landscapes. Some did not settle but crossed over an icy land-bridge from the Chukotka peninsula into America, then making their way southwards: there are still loose connections between the Chukchi people of Northern and Eastern Siberia and the indigenous peoples of the American continent. The Siberian tribes of these regions lived by hunting seals, walrus and whales in the sea, fishing in the rivers, and snaring wild-fowl. In the summer, the season of transhumance, they would lead their reindeer herds up to the higher pastures.

The Russians first began advancing across the Urals in the late sixteenth century. They pressed on across the great rivers, the Ob, Yenisey and Lena, till they eventually arrived on the Pacific Coast, in 1649, and founded Okhotsk. Siberia's attraction lay in its great wealth of fur, in its gold, diamond, silver, iron, copper, lead, salt and timber resources. These eventually led to the growth of local industries and towns and also to the construction of the Trans-Siberian Railway between 1891 and 1905, providing a link between Moscow and Vladivostok. Later, huge reserves of oil and gas were discovered and gigantic hydro-electric power stations were built to harness the mighty Siberian rivers. The Siberian taiga is, nonetheless, still inhabited by 'old-time trappers', men who live by hunting, fishing and gathering, only going to town for salt, and metal fishing and hunting gear.

Siberia and the Far East are home to many small groups of indigenous peoples. The Mongols, who conquered the whole of Russia in the thir-

45. Snow-clad statue of Lenin in the city of Petropavlovsk, the capital of Kamchatka. From the late 1920s, statues of the Bolshevik leader occupied an important place in urban planning throughout Russia. Many have since been pulled down and sold for scrap. Some have become collectors' items.

46. Real Russian cold. Siberia! The town of Oimyakon in north-east Siberia is the coldest inhabited place on earth, with temperatures recorded at more than 70 degrees C. below zero.

47. Mount Kronotskaya (11,579 ft), in the heart of Kamchatka's volcano country, is the second highest mountain on the peninsula, after Klyuchevskaya (15,580 ft), the 'boiling mountain'.

48. *Petropavlovsk-Kamchatsky was founded in 1740 by the celebrated explorer Vitus Bering on Avacha Bay, one of the world's great natural harbours. It became a typical product of the Bolshevik dream to industrialize the Far East: the ugly modern housing, factory chimney and slogan contrast with the magnificent mountain behind.*

49. On the only road to Milkovo, a town 125 mi. north of Petropavlovsk-Kamchatsky. Heavy snow makes communications extra difficult in winter.

50. Even in the bitterest weather children are expected to make their way to school. Only if the temperature drops to minus 50 degrees C. can they stay home.

51. Driving through the countryside in winter is safe only in convoys, since a breakdown could be fatal for a lone motorist. Many cars disappear into garages to await the spring.

52. A helicopter lands in the wilderness of Kamchatka, bringing in visitors and food supplies to the Valley of the Geysers, an extraordinary collection of bubbling mud cauldrons and other thermal displays that was discovered by chance in 1941.

53. *A hilltop view of Petropavlovsk-Kamchatsky. Its founder, the explorer Vitus Bering, named it after his two ships, the St Peter and St Paul,*

54. *The active Koryakskaya volcano (11,342 ft) poses a constant threat to Petropavlovsk's 700,000 inhabitants, but provides a magnificent backdrop for the city, which is an important naval base, home to Russia's Pacific submarine fleet (overleaf).*

55. *Aerial view of Eastern Siberia. River routes were of great importance in the colonization of Siberia. The Russians began advancing eastward in the sixteenth century and in 1649 reached the Pacific. They then carried on across the Bering Strait and took possession of Alaska, which they sold to the United States in 1867.*

56. *Aerial view of Lake Kronotskoye, the largest freshwater lake on Kamchatka, located in the Kronotsky Nature Reserve on the west coast of the peninsula, on the shore of the Bering Sea.*

*57. The Maly Semlyachik volcano (5,120 ft)
in south-east Kamchatka.*

58. *The Koryak mountain range in northern Kamchatka, shrouded in mist.*

59-61. *There are still few tourists in the Valley of the Geysers in the carefully protected Kronotsky Nature Reserve. As there are no roads, the valley has to be reached by helicopter or on foot.*

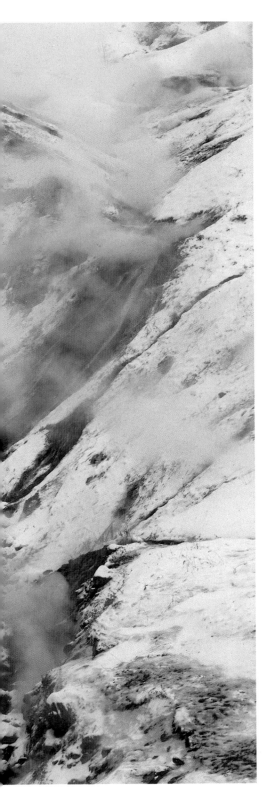

62. Besides being an important navy base,
which accounts for half the number of its
population, Petropavlovsk-Kamchatsky is a
harbour for fishing trawlers. The fishing
industry is vital to the region's economy: a
million tons of fish are caught a year; crab
and salmon are abundant.

63, 64. *Steam rises from the surface of the hot spring, laced with sulphur, heated by the magma at the heart of a nearby volcano. Currents of icy water mix with the warmer swirls, making bathing here an exhilarating experience. The air temperature can be gauged from the fur hat.*

65. The Yerusan River curls like a serpent across Bashkiria (Bashkortostan) before flowing through the capital, Ufa, and joining the Belaya River (882 mi. in length).

66. Young rafters, Russian versions of Tom Sawyer and Huckleberry Finn, on Lake Baikal. The world's most ancient lake (25 million years old) and the deepest (5,315 ft), it contains one fifth of the world's fresh water.

67. The elk (or moose) of northern Siberia. In summer they live near the swamps, rivers and lakes, wading deep into the water to feed on aquatic plants. They are hunted for their meat, though some have been domesticated.

*68. A Russian/Buryat family living in the
north of the Republic of Buryatia, not far
from Lake Baikal. Russians began to settle
in this region as early as the eighteenth
century, and there has been considerable
intermarriage with the native Buryats, a
Mongol people.*

69. *Preserving nature is a primary concern of the father of this family, the director of a national park in Eastern Siberia. There were over 140 state nature reserves in the former Soviet Union, many located in the tundra and forest belts of Russia. Nonetheless, huge chunks of Siberia suffer from industrial pollution.*

70. An old-time trapper from Palana. It was in search of furs that many of the early pioneers made their way across the Urals into Siberia and opened up the country — much like the trappers of North America.

71. Innumerable variations of traditional costume are to be found all over Russia. In the past, embroidery was much appreciated and almost every village had its own patterns. Nowadays such dress is to be seen mostly on festive occasions. These women wear the costume of the Suzdal region.

72. Historically, the Buryats had a horse-centred culture. As part of her dowry, a Buryat girl received a riding horse with all the trappings. If the marriage was dissolved by mutual consent, she had the right to demand one riding horse, and also one summer and one winter costume.

73. *A Buryat woman with her horse near Ulan Ude, capital of the Buryat Republic. The Buryats are a branch of the eastern Mongols — some claim direct descent from Ghenghis Khan.*

74. A Tatar hunter with his German shepherd dog. Sometimes hunters pick up stray wolf cubs and tame them like dogs. There are an estimated 120,000 wolves in Russia, but they are an unprotected species and hunting is thought to be steadily reducing their number.

75. The carved window frame and clay figurines are typical of Siberia. Traditional toys, fashioned out of clay, porcelain, bone or even straw, moss, cloth and dough, were usually brightly painted and depicted figures from folk tales. Clay figurines were dried in the open air before being fired in the family oven and painted with water-soluble pigments dissolved in egg yolk.

76. Workers in Bashkiria, near the southern Ural Mountains. The Bashkirs are a Turkic people, traditionally Muslim by faith. About one million of them live in the Bashkir Republic, a region exceptionally rich in natural resources: oil, gas, timber, and many ores.

77. Chess, one of the most popular pastimes in all parts of Russia, is played by all ages and often out of doors.

78. The Buddhist datsan at Ivoginsk near Ulan Ude, the larger of the two active Buddhist monasteries in Buryatia. The Mongol Buryats, who now number some 400,000, adopted Lamaist Buddhism in the early eighteenth century. In recent years there has been a marked revival of the faith in the republic.

79. *A frosty morning with sunshine sparkling on crisp snow: a cheerful aspect of the severe Russian winter, when no sensible person ventures out without boots and fur hat.*

80. The thaw (ottepel), impatiently awaited after the long, ice-bound winter, swells the rivers and, incidentally, causes widespread flooding. In his novella 'The Thaw', the writer Ilya Ehrenburg used this as a metaphor for Khrushchev's relaxation of political repression following the death of Stalin.

81. A Chukchi mother and child. Life in Chukotka means two months of summer and ten months of severe frost and gale-force winds.

82. A Chukchi of the tundra. In their own national area of Chukotka, in the far north-east of the country, there are some 13,600 Chukchi, who like their neighbours, the Koryak and Itelmen, speak a Paleo-Asiatic language.

83. Chukchi hospitality. Divided into the settled 'coastal' and the nomadic 'reindeer' people, the Chukchi have traditionally made their living by hunting and fishing or reindeer herding.

84, 85. A Chukchi reindeer herder and child. Average life expectancy for this people is 43 years, compared with 72 for the American Eskimo living only a few miles away across the the Bering Strait in Alaska. One of the reasons is poor diet combined with alcoholism.

86. *Anadyr, capital of Chukotka, at the mouth of the River Anadyr where it enters the sea of the same name. In the 1960s many Russians moved to this remote region to develop gold and mineral resources, with the inducement of better pay and housing than in European Russia. Because of the harsh living conditions and weather, large numbers have since returned.*

87. *Like Buddhist prayer flags, the laundry flutters from long lines, raised high to catch the sunlight. An immense amount of time and work, much of it done by women, is needed to keep clean, warm and fed in a society where labour-saving appliances are few and the climate is inhospitable for much of the year.*

*88. A newly-married couple place a bou-
quet on the steps of a statue of Lenin in
Novosibirsk. A hang-over from Soviet
times, the continuation of this custom
shows that attitudes do not change
overnight.*

89. Even when there is no religious ceremony, the Russian bride will often wear a
traditional white gown and have the trappings of a church wedding. Sometimes
more than a hundred guests will gather in
a restaurant for a party at which vodka and
the local 'champagne' flow freely.

90. The dark eyes of this Itelmen girl are half hidden by her fur hat. The Itelmen are descendants of the Paleo-Asiatic inhabitants of the far eastern areas of the country, a group which also includes the Chukchi (the most numerous) and Koryak peoples.

91. An Eskimo (Inuit) girl, not from North America, as might be thought, but from one of several small groups of Eskimos living on the south-east Chukotka coast, where her ancestors fished and hunted sea mammals.

92. Logs are gathered into huge rafts and floated downstream to the sea. Most of the timber from Kamchatka is bound for Japan.

93. Vladivostok, Russia's most important eastern coast port, was for many years a closed city, being one of the main bases of the Soviet Navy.

teenth century, are represented by two small groups, the Buryats, living in the peripheral regions of Siberia, close to Mongolia, and the Kalmyks, who originally came from Western Siberia to settle on the steppes to the west of Astrakhan. The Tungus-Manchurian peoples of Siberia and the Far East include the Evenki (formerly known as the Tungus), who inhabit much of the land between the Yenisey and the Pacific, and many other smaller tribes living in north-east and south-east Siberia. The descendants of the earliest inhabitants of Siberia are probably the Paleo-Asiatic peoples, related to the native North Americans. Paleo-Asiatic languages are spoken by the Chukchi in north-eastern Siberia, and the Koryak, Itelmen, Yukagir and Nivkh groups on the north-east and south-east seaboard. The Ket language is unique, being the last surviving member of the Yenisey family of languages that once stretched all the way to south-west Siberia; the Kets now live along the Yenisey River in Western Siberia.

At the beginning of this century the peoples of Siberia had no written languages, but there were bards who spun fabulous stories to help while away the long winter nights. Families and friends huddled inside cone-shaped tents made out of deerskin or walrus hide, listening to the stories, riddles and tongue-twisters, with the Arctic wind and snowstorms howling outside. In Sakha (Yakutia) the bards, called *olonosuts*, were famous for their recitals of epic poems about the wanderings of a mythical hero, which could continue for as many as five or six evenings in a row. The subjects of Siberian folk tales ranged from the Creation and stories of the spirits to everyday life and animal fables. Their settings were the northern environment, with snowstorms raging across the tundra, the Sun riding through the sky in a golden sledge, and the Northern Lights walking across the ocean.

Western Siberia

The economic region of Western Siberia lies between the Urals and the Yenisey River. Its biggest city, Novosibirsk (over a million inhabitants), which lies on the right bank of the River Ob and its tributaries, the Kamenka and Yeltsovka, is an important railway junction and river port. Novosibirsk is the seat of the Siberian branch of the Russian Academy of Sciences and has an opera house bigger even than Moscow's Bolshoi Theatre. To the east of the city the landscape is dotted with the mining towns of the Kutnetsk coal basin.

Other major cities include Tyumen, the first Siberian town after one crosses the Urals, founded in 1586 and famous for its decorative wooden architecture; Tobolsk, on the River Irtysh, founded as early as 1547, and the supply centre for most of the northern territory of Western Siberia; Omsk, notorious for the prison, dating from the time of Catherine the Great, where Dostoevsky, among others, was incarcerated; and Tomsk, on the River Tom, founded in 1604, which became the first university city of Siberia in 1888, when it was an important centre for gold smelting.

From Novosibirsk by Trans-Siberian express to Krasnoyarsk, capital of the immense territory of the Krasnoyarsky Kray, stretching through central Siberia up to the Arctic coast, the distance is some 560 mi. At this point, the distance to back to Moscow is over 2,500 mi. Krasnoyarsk stands on the banks of the Yenisey, which divides the Western and Eastern Siberian economic regions. 'A mighty, raging giant who does not know what to do with his strength and youth' was how Anton Chekhov described the Yenisey, which flows across Siberia from south to north. It rises in the wooded Sayan Mountains of the Tuva Autonomous Republic, home of the Turkic-speaking native Tuvinians. Kyzyl, Tuva's main city, at the conflu-

94. Though the calm expanse of Lake Baikal seems remote from civilization, it is threatened by industrial pollution from towns such as Irkutsk, capital of the Buryat Republic, and other settlements on its shores. Baikal, in south-eastern Siberia, covers an area of 12,200 sq. mi. and is 395 mi. in length.

ence of the Yenisey and two of its tributaries, is the geographical centre of Asia, as recorded by an obelisk bearing an inscription to this effect written in Russian, Tuvin and English.

Further downstream from Kyzyl is the town of Abakan, capital of the Kharkass Autonomous Region, which is considered the cradle of Siberian civilization because of the burial mounds found there, dating back three to five thousand years. The region around Abakan is mountainous with varied scenery, both steppe and taiga, and many fresh-water and salt lakes.

Eastern Siberia

Between the Yenisey and Lena rivers and north of the Sayan highlands is the mineral-rich economic region of Eastern Siberia, which includes the autonomous republics of Buryatia and Sakha (formerly Yakutia) and one of the world's wonders, Lake Baikal.

Buryatia, curving in a sickle around the eastern and northern shores of Lake Baikal and bordering on Mongolia, is part mountainous landscape with pine and larch forests, part steppe land, where cattle, horses and sheep are raised. Its capital and main industrial city, Ulan-Ude (formerly Verkhneudinsk), originated in 1666 as a Cossack wintering fortress at the confluence of the rivers Uda and Selenga, which flow into Lake Baikal. A Mongol people who made their home in the rugged mountains near Baikal long before Ghenghis Khan swept through, the Buryats found themselves on the Russian side of the frontier with Mongolia (then China) when it was drawn in 1727. The Autonomous Republic of Buryatia was created in 1923.

To the north of Buryatia, on the other side of Lake Baikal, stands the pleasant town of Irkutsk on the River Angara. Founded in 1652, it is one of the most important administrative centres of Eastern Siberia. The streets are wide, laid out on a grid system and lined with eighteenth- and nineteenth-century wooden houses, so that the sky-line is low. A place of historic interest is the Decembrist Museum, a lovely mansion in a quiet back street, elegantly furnished and with one room devoted to correspondence by and photographs of the Decembrists, who were sent into exile for conspiring against the Tsar in 1825. Siberia had been a place of exile since 1648, and became a land of banishment for political prisoners in 1729. By 1891 it was estimated that 100,000 Polish rebels, 40,000 Russian criminals, 50,000 Russian political exiles and 5,000 wives who had chosen to follow their husbands, were in exile in Siberia.

Hundreds of miles away to the north-east of Irkutsk is the Sakha Autonomous Republic (formerly Yakutia), a region of vast natural resources, covering over 1.2 million sq. mi. — almost the size of India. The main wealth of the republic is a treasure trove of diamonds: it yields a quarter by weight of the world's total output (12 million carats a year). One giant diamond, weighing 241.8 carats, was named 'Free Russia' in 1992, to mark the collapse of the Soviet Union. Extracting the diamonds is not easy as Sakha is one of the coldest inhabited regions of the world: winter temperatures tend to drop to 45 degrees C. below zero.

The republic is the homeland of the Turkic-speaking Yakut people, who have certain similarities with the Indians of Peru. Their traditional occupations are hunting, fishing and raising cattle. As craftsmen they are noted for their bone carvings: delicately fashioned boxes, pipes, chessmen and dagger hilts, which were exported from the eighteenth century on. The principal town of the region, Yakutsk (pop. 140,000), stands on the left bank of the River Lena, one of the world's longest rivers. It is up to six mi. wide in places and freezes in winter to a depth of over seven ft. Not inappropriately, one of the town's main attractions is the Museum of Perma-Frost.

The Far East

Beyond the Lena, the demarcation line between Eastern Siberia and the Far East, the Siberian plain turns into rugged, mountainous terrain. A region of striking contrasts, the Far East Economic Region has a coastline of 5,600 mi. and a large fishing industry. It extends from the Arctic tundra of the Chukotka and Koryak districts in the north to the lush monsoon forests of the Kamchatka peninsula and Ussuriland in the south. Of particular interest for its wild life is Wrangel Island, a nature reserve off the coast of Chukotka, the north-eastern tip of the country. The mountainous island, named after Ferdinand Wrangel, a Russian explorer, is a refuge for more than two hundred breeding polar bears, schools of walrus, herds of hardy musk ox and colonies of snow geese.

Chukotka is the home of the Chukchi, numbering only about 13,600, who speak a Paleo-Asiatic language. From this and other indications, it is probable that long ago they migrated here from somewhere far to the south. There are no snakes in any part of north-eastern Siberia, but in Chukchi folklore, a description of a boa-constrictor appears: a red-striped serpent, capable of attacking a wild reindeer, crushing it in its coils, swallowing it whole, and falling asleep afterwards.

South of Chukotka is the Kamchatka peninsula, a wilderness of forest overlooked by smoking volcanoes. The economy revolves around salmon fishing, oil and coal extraction, and mercury and silver mining. The main city is Petropavlovsk-Kamchatka, founded in 1740 on the Bering Sea coast. The indigenous people, the Kamchadals, were described by the French explorer, Jean de Lesseps, who travelled from Kamchatka across Siberia to St Petersburg and thence to Paris in 1787. He recorded them as being 'in general below the common height; their shape is round and squat, their eyes small and sunk, their cheeks prominent, their nose flat, their hair black; they have scarcely any beard, and their complexion is a little tawny...'

The offshore Sakhalin Island, further south again, was described as 'a perfect hell' by Anton Chekhov, who spent three months studying conditions in the penal colony there, in a letter dated 9 December 1890. Its gloomy, foggy and wet climate may have contributed to this impression. Sakhalin has considerable investment potential owing to its reserves of oil, gas and minerals, and abundance of crab and salmon. Ever since it was declared a joint Russian-Japanese possession in 1855, it has been a bone of contention between the two countries. In 1875 the whole island was taken by the Russians, who used it as a vast penal colony, but in 1905 the southern part reverted to Japan. Since 1945 the island has belonged to Russia. The native inhabitants, the Ainu, worshipped their ancestors and the forces of nature, and practised ritual bear sacrifices.

Ussuriland, in the southern part of the Russian Far East, has lush, jungle-like, monsoon forests, where the rare Amur leopard and Siberian tiger pad through the undergrowth, surprising the wild boar which they feed upon. In the Khanka lowlands of Ussuriland, there are meadows, marshes, rice paddies and expanses of open water, while forests of maple, Amur cork, Mongolian oak and Amur linden clothe the foothills of the Sikhote Alin range (average height 3,300 ft). Delicate pink rhododendrons, magnolias, exotic orange irises, lilies, orchids and other brilliantly coloured wild flowers are an attraction of the Cedar Ravine nature reserve in the very south, a few miles from the North Korean and Chinese borders.

Khabarovsk, a major road, rail and river transport centre of the Far East, is situated on the Amur in the Ussuri lowlands. From here the great river turns west and for much of its course forms the border between Russia and China. The city was named after the seventeenth-century Russian explorer, Yerofei Khaborov, whose monument stands in the square by the railway station. Not far distant is the Jewish Autonomous Oblast, tucked away amidst the woods and meadows of the middle Amur valley. In 1934 the area was designated a Jewish homeland, but it attracted few settlers and the population is not predominantly Jewish. The main city is Birobidzhan, a stop on the Trans-Siberian Railway.

Next in importance after Khabarovsk is Vladivostok ('Master of the East'), founded in 1860 and built with the use of Chinese labour. A kind of Russian Penzance, it stands at the end of a short peninsula, overlooking the Sea of Japan, some 4,350 mi. away from Moscow. Climbing the slopes of hills above a bay, the city is the main Pacific port and naval base for the Pacific fleet, and the terminus of the Trans-Siberian Railway.

The inadequacy of communications between European Russia and the Far East were demonstrated during the Russo-Japanese War at the beginning of the century, when the Trans-Siberian Railway, the only railway crossing from west to east, proved incapable of transporting sufficient numbers of troops across the enormous distance. As a result, an expedition was dispatched from Vladivostok to explore another east-west route, through the Arctic Ocean. It was during the expedition to navigate a northern sea route between 1910 and 1913 that the previously mentioned, hitherto uncharted Severnaya Zemlya (Northern Lands) Islands were discovered. They were duly annexed to the immense Russian Empire, the creation of which will be the subject of the next few chapters.

Summer and winter dwellings of Kamchadals, nineteenth-century engraving.

KIEVAN RUS AND MUSCOVY

Every country has a golden age. In the case of Russia, it began in the ninth century A.D. with the founding of the state called Kievan Rus, a loose confederation of principalities under a grand prince. At the peak of its might, it encompassed the vast Russian plain bounded by the Ural Mountains in the east, the Black Sea in the south, the Carpathian Mountains in the west, and the Baltic Sea in the north. As in all golden ages, there were fair and mighty knights in Rus. These knights or *bogatyrs* were like the knights of Arthurian legend, and their Camelot was the city of Kiev on the River Dnieper.

But long before this age there were Slavs living on the territory of Russia, alongside many other peoples. Their origin is unknown, though some scholars believe that they moved north from the Caucasus to settle in the areas between the great rivers Vistula and Don, where they were established in separate groups by at least 800 B.C.

From about the eighth century B.C. on, pressure from the Chinese drove waves of nomadic tribes westward. Among them were the Scythians, an Iranian-Altaian nomadic people, who settled in what is now southern Russia, in the area between the Caspian Sea and the Carpathians. They were renowned horsemen, whose use of the saddle, when the Greeks were still riding bareback, gave them military superiority. Famous also as goldsmiths, they were described by the Greek historian, Herodotus. After the Greeks founded their colonies on the Black Sea shores from about 700 B.C., there was considerable trade between the two peoples.

The Scythian-ruled lands included areas previously settled by the Slavs, some of whom moved further north. In the second century B.C. the Scythians were displaced by another Iranian nomadic people, the Sarmatians, who were later defeated by Emperor Trajan: images of these distant barbarians adorn his victory column in civilized Rome. They, in turn, were overrun, some four centuries later, by the Goths, a Baltic people, who swept away the Sarmatians, completing Trajan's work, and extended their territory to the Black Sea. Most of the Slavs had recognized the Goths as overlords by A.D. 400, by which time the Huns had appeared on the scene. Under Attila, they established an empire stretching from the Rhine to the Caspian Sea, and the Slavs found themselves with new overlords.

In those turbulent times, waves of new invaders continually swept in from the east, but none of them held the territories they overran for any length of time. When Hunnish power declined in the latter half of the fifth century and the Germanic tribes started moving further west, the Slavs began spreading out, reaching as far as the Elbe. Around the middle of the sixth century, another Mongol people, the Avars, established a khanate from the Elbe to the Don. After half a century this, too, had disintegrated, though a reduced Avar khanate survived well into the seventh century in the middle and lower Danube region. The Avars are recorded as inflicting defeats on the Slavs who had begun penetrating into Byzantine territory in the Balkans.

Between the sixth and tenth centuries, during the period of great migrations of peoples, the Slavs began splitting into three main groups or branches: the western, southern and eastern. It is from the eastern Slavs that the Russians are descended. As a result of intermingling with the Finnic tribes who earlier occupied the Russian heartland and Turkic peoples, in general their physical appearance, with high cheek-bones and small eyes, differs somewhat from that of the western and southern Slavs.

In earliest times, the Slavs, organized into clans and tribes, were nomadic pastoralists. They called themselves Slovene or Sloviane, which probably derives from *slovo* meaning 'the word', to signify people with the gift of speech, as distinct from foreigners, who were named 'the dumb' or *nemtsy*, meaning, presumably, that their speech was unintelligible! When they began to lead a more settled life in villages, in the forest regions they practised the 'slash-burn' type of agriculture, whereby they cleared glades and used the ashes from the burnt tree stumps and brush as fertilizer, and moved on again when the soil became exhausted after a few good harvests. Since the soil in the northern parts was mostly poor and the climate unfavourable to agriculture, to supplement their income, the Slavs engaged in other occupations called *promysly*, by which they exploited the resources of the forest: its furs, honey, and the fish in the rivers.

The various tribal communities mostly lived scattered around a stockade, an earthen or wooden fortification, where they would take shelter in times of danger. The tribal groups were linked by the worship of common gods: near Lake Onega, for example, they celebrated religious rites in pine groves, believing that trees could cure by their touch, as the bark had healing properties. Local gods, such as Perun, the God of Thunder and Creator of Fire, and the bright-plumed firebird of Russian fairy tales and Stravinsky's ballet were also worshipped.

Many of the Slavs recognized the overlordship of their neighbours, the Khazars, a Turkic people who had settled in the sixth century on the shores of the Caspian. In the seventh and eighth centuries the Khazars ruled over an empire (kaganate) stretching from the Volga to the Urals and incorporating in its north-western part territory settled by Slavs. The empire's capital, Itil, on the lower Volga, was a trade centre between Asia and Europe and a hive of many different peoples: Khazars, Greeks, Georgians, Christians, Muslims and Jews. The Khazars converted to Judaism in the eighth century, but other religions were tolerated, as demonstrated by the balanced composition of their Supreme Court, which included two Muslims, one Jew, one Christian, and one heathen judge for the Slavs. Under the Khazar kaganate's protection, as many as six hundred Slav settlements grew into trading posts.

The Golden Age

The name of Rus was given to the land of the Slavs in the ninth century. The origin of the term is disputed, but it probably derives from *ruotsi*, a Finnish word for the Vikings, the Norsemen who attacked the Slavs when the Khazar kaganate was destroyed by Asiatic hordes. Conquerors also of Ireland, Iceland, and Normandy, the Vikings, otherwise known as Varangians or Varangarians, penetrated south into the Slav lands along the rivers Dnieper and Volga, settled, and soon subjugated the Slav population, from whom they exacted tribute, though they would quickly become Slavicized. In 862 the Varangian ruler, Rurik (862-79), founder of the Rurikid dynasty, captured the busy northern town of Novgorod on the River Volkhov. Rurik's younger son, Oleg, would take Smolensk, Lyubech and Kiev in 882.

When Oleg, nicknamed the Prophetic, sat on the throne of Kiev, he declared: 'This will be the mother of the cities of Rus,' according to an early Russian chronicle. Kiev, which he fortified and made into his capital, was well placed on the principal trading waterway between the Gulf of Finland and the Bosphorus, referred to as 'the Great Way from the Varangians to the Greeks'. Every summer Varangian and Slav merchants loaded up their boats with cargoes of furs, wax, honey, amber and slaves, and travelled downstream to Constantinople. Trading conditions were favourable. Provided they refrained from looting and did not appear in markets in groups of more than fifty, the Varangians and Slavs had assurances from the Byzantines of food and accommodation, as well as supplies of sails and anchors for the journey home. Besides Kiev, other towns grew up; Rostov, Suzdal, Novgorod and Pskov, where trade was flourishing, set high standards in architecture and painting.

As a result of its contacts with Constantinople, then the greatest city of Christendom, Rus had become permeated with Christian culture. In 988 the recently converted Prince Vladimir of Kiev (978-1015) proclaimed Christianity as the official religion and the whole population of Kiev was forcibly baptized in the waters of the River Dnieper. A famous story tells why Vladimir decided to adopt Christianity: Islam was rejected as a possible option because it prohibited alcohol, even though paradise sounded promising; the better choice was the Greek Church, for its rituals had an unforgettable beauty and sweetness which, once tasted, made it impossible for the person to remain a pagan.

Perhaps more relevant were the political advantages of conversion which, combined with trade links, enabled Rus to emerge as an acknowledged European power. As Christians, the princesses of Rus could form matrimonial alliances with the reigning families of Europe. In the eleventh century, the children of Prince Yaroslav the Wise made matches with royal and noble families of Germany, Poland, Norway, Hungary and France, while he himself married a princess of Sweden.

Another important consequence was the adoption of a literary language, Church Slavonic, which used a script based on Greek with extra letters for Russian sounds, devised by Byzantine missionaries. This paved the way for the flowering of Kievan culture that came under Yaroslav the Wise (1019-54). This was also the age of intensive church building that produced the great cathedrals of St Sophia (1037-39) in Kiev and St Demetrius (1194) in Vladimir. Western travellers of the eleventh century admired the

View of Izmailovo, Moscow, engraving by I.F. Zubov, 1728-9.

127

hundreds of churches in Kiev and noted the eight great markets. The cosmopolitan court read and enjoyed books and was familiar with foreign languages. In the monasteries, especially in the famous Pecherskaya Lavra, learned monks translated Greek and transcribed old Slavonic books. Under Yaroslav the Wise, the first written code of Russian laws called *Russkaya Pravda* was issued.

During the twelfth century, the distant world of Rus approached a crisis. One cause was the impractical rule of succession inaugurated by Yaroslav. On his death in 1054, the division of the realm among his sons led to warfare among the princes and the fragmentation of the territory of Kievan Rus into some dozen small states, mostly named after the chief city of each. Grand Prince Vladimir Monomakh briefly reunited the land early in the twelfth century, but it again split apart. The rivalries and conflicts between the principalities throughout the following century made them easy prey for the Mongols, who conquered all the Russian states except Novgorod by 1241.

Another factor contributing to the crisis was the decline of trade after Constantinople was seized by the Crusaders in 1204, and because steppe nomads, such as the Polovtsians, never ceased attacking the flotillas with their cargoes as they travelled downstream. Only the northernmost Russian region, the Republic of Novgorod, which had become self-governing in 997 and completely independent of Kievan Rus in 1136, enjoyed a greater degree of economic prosperity. In the meantime, other enemies, the Teutonic Knights, the Lithuanians, Swedes and Hungarians, threatened from the West.

To escape the dangers and uncertainties caused by the constant feuding among the princes, the population started fleeing to the wooded northwest in the area of the upper Volga and the basin of the River Oka. In 1169 Kiev was sacked by a group of twelve Slav princes led by Prince Andrei Bogolyubsky, who established Vladimir as his new capital in the north-west and took the title of grand prince. After his murder in 1175, he was succeeded as grand prince by his brother, Vsevolod, who held the confederation together until his death in 1212. Again conflicts broke out among the princes, to be cut short by the invasion of the Mongol hordes.

Destruction was swift. The Mongols, who had come through Persia and Georgia, riding along the sandy shores of the Caspian, appeared like a black cloud on the steppe north of the Caucasus Mountains. From there they advanced, defeating a joint force of Russians and Polovtsians at the battle of the River Kalka in 1223. Having swept through Russia and the Ukraine, they mysteriously retired and were not seen for the next decade. They reappeared, however, under Batu Khan, one of Ghengis Khan's grandsons, to whom the Great Khan had bequeathed leadership of the tribes of the Golden Horde. After plundering the lands of the Kama Bulgars on the middle Volga, the Golden Horde marched on the town of Ryazan in 1236. Ryazan and nearly all the cities of eastern Rus were captured and their inhabitants massacred. Batu Khan was unable to reach Novgorod, Smolensk and Pskov, as his army of horsemen floundered in the marshy forests around these towns, so instead he turned south, sacking Pereyaslavl and Chernigov. In 1240 his forces totally devastated Kiev and by 1241 the towns and principalities of Rus had lost their independence.

After the fall of Kievan Rus, its lost glory was lamented in folklore and legend. The *byliny* or folk ballads tell how the knights of Rus 'grew weak and turned to stone, running to the stone mountains, to the dark caves' as they tried to escape the overwhelming Mongol army, and how since then there had been no more heroes in the land of Rus.

96. St Basil's Cathedral on Red Square was built by Ivan the Terrible to commemorate Muscovy's conquest of the khanate of Kazan in the 1550s. Inspired by the shapes of Russian timber churches, it is of suitably festive appearance, enhanced by the colourful paint work added in the seventeenth century. Officially dedicated to the feast of the Intercession of the Virgin (Pokrov), it is popularly called after the 'holy fool' Basil (Vassily), who was buried in its walls soon after its completion.

97. *View of the Kremlin at night from the Moskva River, with the Annunciation Tower in the foreground and the Great Palace (1838-49) to the right, overlooked by the Ivan Veliky bell tower. A fortress (kreml) has existed on the site since the twelfth century, when Prince Yury Dolgoruky raised a wooden fortification here. In the fifteenth century Ivan the Great commissioned four Italian architects to rebuild the Kremlin in stone.*

98. *Cupolas like golden chessmen on the roof of the Terem Palace within the Kremlin (overleaf). The palace, mostly seventeenth-century but with some much older parts, contains the private apartments of the first Romanov tsars, Michael and his son Alexis, as well as a number of chapels.*

99. The Ukraine Hotel, on the left bank of the Moskva River facing the White House, is an example of 1950s Stalinist architecture, one of the city's eight famous 'wedding cakes', resembling latter-day Gothic cathedrals. Though their style was much scorned at the time by western critics, they have weathered better than much twentieth-century architecture.

100. Some of the imposing mansions of the aristocracy and merchant princes were turned into museums after the Revolution. This is the Timairiazev Biological Museum on Moscow's Malaya Gruzinskaya Street.

101. One of the cannon captured from Napoleon in 1812 that are now ranged along the Kremlin wall beside the Arsenal. Appropriately snow-covered, it recalls the disastrous winter retreat that decimated the French Grand Army after its capture of Moscow. When two-thirds of the city were burnt down and the army was left without food supplies, the Emperor had no option but to withdraw.

102. *Lavrushensky Lane in the snow with magnificent wrought-iron work, more typical of St Petersburg than Moscow. In tsarist times, Russian craftsmen were famous for metalworking, whether making weapons, casting bells or creating exquisite jewellery and objets d'art, such as the Fabergé Easter eggs.*

103. Rozhdestvensky Boulevard with examples of the neo-classical style of architecture popular in the early nine- teenth century, when Moscow was rebuilt following the great fire of 1812 during the Napoleonic War. At that time, many of the traditional wooden houses destroyed in the fire were replaced by stone buildings.

104. *The Museum of the Revolution (formerly the English Club) was originally built in 1780 as a private mansion, used by Tolstoy as the model for the house of Pierre Bezukhov in his 'War and Peace'. Reconstructed after the 1812 fire by the English architect Adam Menelaws, it was turned into a club modelled on London gentlemen's clubs and became a popular meeting place for the nobility. Lev Tolstoy is said to have lost a thousand roubles there in one night playing cards.*

*105. The colourful Petrovsky (Peter) Palace
was built (1776-82) by Catherine the Great
on the outskirts of Moscow as a place
where she could rest before entering the
city after the exhausting journey by car-
riage from St Petersburg. Its architect,
Matvei Kazakov, employed an odd mixture
of traditional Russian and Gothic elements
to create a most original building, in which
Napoleon stayed briefly in 1812 to escape
the burning city.*

106. The Maly (Small) Theatre on Sverdlova Street (1821-24) was designed by Osip Bove, the chief architect in charge of the reconstruction of Moscow after the fire. In front stands the statue of the celebrated nineteenth-century playwright Alexander Ostrovsky (1823-86). Nearby is the Bolshoi (Big) Theatre.

107. The wooden palace of Ostankino, now a museum, was designed by Italian architects in the late eighteenth century. A gift from the immensely wealthy Count Nikolai Sheremetiev to his mistress, later his wife, the actress Praskovia Zhemchugova, it included a private theatre that could be transformed by mechanical means into a ballroom.

108. The Bolshoi Theatre, founded in 1776, is Moscow's oldest and most renowned home of opera and ballet. The present structure, which can seat over 2,000, was built by architect Albert Cavos after the previous theatre on this site, the work of Osip Bove, burnt down in 1853.

109. The Gate Church of the
Transfiguration (Preobrazhenskaya) at
Novodevichy (New Maidens) Convent,
founded in 1524. To this convent Peter the
Great banished both his half-sister and
rival, the Regent Sophia, and his first wife,
Evdokia.

110. Iconostasis of the Annunciation
Cathedral (Blagoveshchensky Sobor) in the
Moscow Kremlin, painted in the early fif-
teenth century by three masters of icon
painting: Theophanes the Greek, Andrei
Rublev and Prokhor of Gorodets.

The Mongol Yoke

The shock of the Mongol invasion has never been forgotten: scenes of the raiding and plundering were vividly portrayed in Tarkovsky's famous film *Andrei Rublev* on the life of the Russian icon painter under Mongol rule. Six years after the sack of Kiev, an emissary of the Pope passing through the southern Russian lands saw everywhere traces of fire and mounds of human bones and skulls. Only two hundred houses were left standing in Kiev, formerly one of the most populous cities of medieval Europe. Other towns were burned to the ground and never fully recovered from the catastrophe that had suddenly overtaken them.

The Mongols or Tatars, as they are often called, were a confederation of clans who came from Mongolia. At the height of their power they controlled a vast empire stretching from China to Eastern Europe. Having destroyed Kiev, they moved westwards, through Poland and Hungary, and would probably have conquered western Europe as well had it not chanced that in the summer of 1242, while Batu Khan was encamped in Hungary, news arrived of the death of his uncle, the Great Khan Ogetai, whereupon he headed back to Mongolia for the election of a successor. When Batu and the Golden Horde returned, they did not push further west but established their capital at Sarai on the middle Volga, whence they directly ruled or were overlords of almost all Russian lands down to 1480.

Mongol rule was Russia's first experience of a strong, centralized government organized on the principle that everything must be subordinated to the smooth working of the empire, and every man should serve the khan with absolute obedience. Power was unscrupulously and cruelly exercised. The death penalty, which had not existed in Kievan Rus, was introduced. Without actually settling in most parts of Russia (they did not feel at home in the forests, preferring the open steppe), the Mongols imposed *yassak* or heavy tributes on the Slav population, entrusting its collection to the native princes. Except when they went out on raiding expeditions, Mongol officials had scarcely any direct contact with ordinary people. On the other hand, the local princes who were to collect the *yassak* were expected to travel to the Mongol capital at Sarai, or even to Karakorum in Mongolia, to receive a charter of investiture or *yarlyk*. They would have to adopt oriental robes, undergo a ritual of passing between flames, and use all their powers of persuasion to conciliate the khan, as well as spending large sums on gifts for the khan's wife and kinsmen and all the principal grandees of the administration.

The Rise of Muscovy under Ivan the Great

111. Assumption (Uspensky) Cathedral in the Kremlin with the early sixteenth-century Ivan Veliky bell tower behind. The oldest of the Kremlin cathedrals, it was built (1475-79) by the Italian architect, Fioravanti, on the site of an earlier church and was used for royal weddings and coronations.

The tribes of the Golden Horde, converts to Islam, were tolerant of other religions, perhaps because of their conviction that every religion disposed of powerful supernatural forces which it was best to conciliate. In consequence, the Orthodox Church alone survived from the older, more civilized Russia. This fact immensely strengthened its hold on the minds and emotions of the people: under the Mongol yoke, the Russian Church entered its heyday. Thanks to the exemption of the clergy from the tribute imposed on the rest of the population, the Church also grew rich. In the 1320s, it moved its administration from Vladimir to the up-and-coming town of Moscow.

The insignificant fortified village of Moscow, founded in the first half of the twelfth century, gradually gained in importance in the latter half of the thirteenth century to become the centre of a principality, and eventually the pivot of the Russian Empire. Muscovy steadily expanded its territory until it gained supremacy over all the other Russian principalities, though still a Tatar vassal state. One reason for this was its geographically favourable position on the river trade route between the Baltic and the Caspian seas that made it a strong commercial centre. Another was the ability of its rulers to collaborate more successfully than the other princes with the khans of the Golden Horde. Moscow's prestige was further enhanced when the metropolitan of the Orthodox Church moved his seat there at about the same time.

Moscow's princes were descended from Daniel (1263-1303), youngest son of the famous Prince Alexander Nevsky of Novgorod who defeated the Teutonic Knights in the celebrated battle on frozen Lake Peipus. It was Daniel who raised Moscow to the level of a principality and started acquiring neighbouring land. After Daniel, Prince Ivan I Kalita (or 'Moneybags', 1325-41), described by Karl Marx as 'the Tatar's ... slave-in-chief', was the first Moscow prince to be granted the right to collect the tribute money from the other Russian principalities. He was followed by Prince Dmitry Donskoi, victor of the battle of Kulikovo over the Mongols in 1380. But the triumph was short-lived: two years later the Mongols returned in force and utterly devastated Moscow, Vladimir and other towns. They remained a threat, though gradually diminishing in strength, for the next one hundred years.

In 1462 Ivan III, described by a Venetian traveller as 'tall, lean and handsome', succeeded to the throne. By the end of his reign, the Mongol yoke had been lifted, the territory of Muscovy had increased fourfold, and he had earned himself the title of Ivan the Great.

Ivan's conquests expanded Muscovy northwards to Tver and further to Novgorod, which he subjugated in 1487. In addition, a number of border territories were wrested from Lithuania. It was during his reign that the Mongols were decisively defeated at the battle of the River Ugra in 1480 and their dominance was finally ended. By 1502 the Golden Horde, already weakened by the campaigns of the Turkic conqueror, Tamerlane, ceased to exist as a united force.

The Kremlin, Moscow: Ivan Veliky Tower and the Imperial Bell, 1856.

146

By now Muscovy was ambitious to establish closer contacts with foreign lands. In 1472 Ivan had strengthened his position by marrying, as his second wife, Sophia Paleologus, niece of the last Byzantine emperor, who had fled from Constantinople when it fell to the Ottoman Turks and was now living in Rome. Though Sophia, when she arrived, proved to be enormously fat, and the Church was hostile to the union because of her Roman upbringing, the marriage was solemnized without delay and Ivan profited by adopting the prestigious Byzantine emblem of the double-headed eagle. Already Ivan saw Muscovy as an imperial power: texts were propagated in order to give the dynasty a Roman pedigree and Byzantine regalia. In the meantime, to transform Moscow into a fitting capital a huge building programme was undertaken, involving the reconstruction of the Kremlin. The results were so impressive that, after the fall of Constantinople, a monk from Pskov writing to Ivan's son, Vassily III, would refer to Moscow as the Third Rome: 'Two Romes have already fallen, but the third remains standing and a fourth there will not be.'

When Ivan died in 1505, the power of Muscovy was consolidated by his successor, Vassily III, who annexed the principalities of Pskov (1510), Ryazan (1517) and Smolensk (1514). In domestic affairs Vassily, like his father before him, was a complete autocrat who decided all matters concerning the lives and property of his subjects. For disobedience to his orders, he imprisoned a boyar (nobleman) who was his own brother-in-law, and caused another to be beheaded for complaining. The Grand Prince divorced his first wife, with whom he had lived for twenty childless years, and married another, who produced a son who has gone down in history as Ivan Grozny ('the Menacing' or 'the Terrible').

Ivan the Terrible and the Time of Troubles

On Vassily's death in 1533, his son and heir, Ivan, was only three years old, so power passed into the hands of his widow, Elena Glinskaya, a Lithuanian princess. She died five years later, perhaps a victim of poison. After that the various aristocratic factions manoeuvred for the right to use Ivan as their pawn until, on a bitter January day in 1547, he was crowned 'Tsar and Autocrat of All the Russias' in the Cathedral of the Assumption in the Moscow Kremlin.

Ivan's first achievement would be to expand Muscovy as far south as the Caspian Sea by the conquest of the Tatar khanates of Kazan and Astrakhan. The victory at Kazan in 1552 was celebrated by the construction of the colourful Pokrova Cathedral, more usually called St Basil's, on Red Square. Ivan also ordered a magnificent new crown, nicknamed the 'Kazan Hat', now displayed in the Kremlin Museum. Made out of gold filigree, with turquoise, pearls, rubies and topazes, its shape imitates the contours of St Basil's Cathedral.

The conquest of Kazan, followed by that of Astrakhan in 1556, was a turning point in Russian history. Not only had Russia gained control of the whole of the Volga region and of Bashkiria, to the east of the Volga, with its Turkic population, but it also found an open gateway, along the Kama River, to Siberia, with its enormous wealth of furs and mineral resources. The military advance into Siberia began with the campaign of Yermak, represented in many songs and pictures as a piratical figure with a black beard and clear brown eyes. Yermak was a hetman ('headman') of the Cossacks (from the Turkic word *kazak* meaning 'rebel'), descendants of peasants who had fled from authority to the frontier region of the Ukraine.

For the most part ethnic Russians, the Cossacks, grouped into armed bands, each under its own leader (ataman or hetman), had traditionally guarded Russia's frontiers against the Poles and the Tatars, with whom there was considerable intermarriage. This tough, frontier breed who liked a life of adventure made excellent pioneers to open up the vast, mostly unexplored wilderness to the east.

Yermak and his Cossack band of some eight hundred men advanced over the Ural Mountains into the Ob river basin of Western Siberia, and defeated the last Tatar defences of the blind Khan Kuchum of Sibir in a battle on the bank of the Irtysh in 1582. In reward, Ivan the Terrible presented Yermak with an ill-fated suit of armour: weighed down by the heavy metal, Yermak later drowned while trying to cross a river after being wounded. As a result of Yermak's campaign, Russians gained control of the entire region of Western Siberia. They set up defences along the river banks in the form of a series of wooden forts (*ostrogi*), around which villages and later towns grew up. Tyumen, the 'mother of Siberian cities', was founded in 1586, followed in 1632 by Yakutsk, and in 1661 by Irkutsk on the River Angara. By this time another Cossack, Dezhnev, had unwittingly sailed through the strait between Asia and America to reach Alaska, later to become a Russian colony, sold to the United States in 1867.

Ivan's reign, which had started so promisingly with military victories and territorial gains, ended in tragedy. Contemporaries attributed the change in the Tsar's character in the middle of his reign to the sudden death in 1560 of his first wife, Anastasia Zakharina, whom Ivan believed had been poisoned. In the year of his wife's death, Ivan threatened abdication, moving to the Alexandrovskaya Monastery about 80 miles north of the capital, but the Moscow populace followed him. The whole procession fell to its knees in the snow before the Tsar, entreating him to return to Moscow (as memorably depicted in Eisenstein's film *Ivan the Terrible*).

When he returned to Moscow, Ivan embarked on a plan to strengthen the autocracy, becoming the scourge of the boyars, the landed aristocracy who held court ranks and were allowed to participate in court and governmental affairs. He divided the country into two parts - the *oprichnina* under his personal rule, and the *zemshchina* under the Council of the Boyars. The *oprichnina* was, in fact, an independent state, the private property of the Tsar, created by expropriating over a seven-year period most of the land north of Moscow and even certain parts of Moscow and Novgorod. Having dispossessed some 12,000 landowners, he settled 6,000 of his own supporters on their estates. Some of boyars who lost their family estates were granted in exchange land as fiefs in other parts of the country. Thus, at one fell swoop, he acquired great personal wealth and patronage and destroyed the economic power of a large section of the boyars. When this had been achieved, the *oprichnina* was abolished in 1572.

To carry through his plans, he formed a hooded order of vigilantes, forerunner of the secret police, named the *oprichniki*, who were held responsible for detecting any signs of treason among the boyars. Dressed in black, mounted on black horses, with a dog's skull on their saddle bow, the *oprichniki* were released into the countryside to commit pillage and murder. In all, some 4,000 boyars were massacred. Other victims were the people of Novgorod, who were suspected of hatching a plot with the Poles, Muscovy's old enemies: almost the entire population of the city was slaughtered in 1570.

As part of his campaign against the boyars, Ivan also destroyed the concept of *mestnichestvo*, whereby each boyar was installed for all time in his inherited position, and deprived them of the right to move abroad or transfer their allegiance elsewhere. He also increased the number of *pomeshchiki*, the gentry whose tenure of land was dependent on service to the state. All this had far-reaching and dire consequences for the ordinary people, the peasantry: as a result of the shortage of labour caused, in part, by the massacres by the *oprichniki*, they lost their freedom to move from one employer to another and became bound serfs.

In 1571 disaster struck the people of Moscow, when an army of 200,000 Crimean Tatar horsemen descended upon the unprepared city. At the moment of crisis, Ivan took fright and decided to flee northwards with his *oprichniki*. If necessary, he was ready to board a ship for England, with whom he had amicable trade relations thanks to the adventurous English sea captain, Richard Chancellor, who had discovered a northern maritime route to Russia. For two years there was no sign of Ivan in the capital, while a ship was kept at Vologda in constant readiness for his flight. Only when the Crimean Tatars retreated, did the Tsar return to Moscow.

Next, after twenty years of war with Sweden, with access to the Baltic as the main objective, in 1582 Ivan had to concede defeat to the Swedes' superior military might. As this example shows, while Russia had found it easy to expand eastwards where military technology was on a fairly primitive level, it was no match for the more advanced technology of the West. A Russian outlet on the Baltic would have to wait until the campaigns of Peter the Great.

In the same year, in a fit of rage, Ivan murdered his eldest son by a blow from his staff during a quarrel when the Tsar had punished his pregnant wife for being too lightly clad. Ivan donated 5,000 roubles to pay for memorial services for his son, but it was said that the tragedy overshadowed the remaining two years of his life: 'Nothing could cheer him up, not drinking with the *oprichniki*, nor songs of the conquest of Kazan and Astrakhan.' He himself died in 1584, while preparing to play a game of chess. Despite his great achievements in expanding the empire, there could have been few who mourned his passing.

View of the Kremlin from the Moskva River, mid-nineteenth century.

Ivan was succeeded by his weak-minded second son, Fedor, who was unfit to govern; the regent and real ruler of the country was the boyar Boris Godunov, his brother-in-law. As the Tsar's younger brother, Dmitry, had been murdered in 1591, allegedly on the orders of Boris Godunov, when Fedor died without issue in 1598, the ancient Rurikid line died with him. Boris Godunov, who had acquitted himself well as regent, was then elected to the Russian throne, but his reign, lasting until 1605, ushered in the chaotic epoch of Russian history known as the 'Time of Troubles'.

Godunov, continuing the policies of Ivan the Terrible, had to suppress several rebellions and faced outside threats to the country's stability, but had time (one of his best-intentioned actions) to send 30 selected future leaders of Russia to study in the West. However, when they were summoned back to their country, all except two failed to reappear, mindful perhaps of the contemporary proverbs: 'Near the Tsar, near death'; 'Everything that is mine belongs to the Tsar'; and 'Fear not the judgement but the judge.' In 1605 the Poles raised an army and marched on Moscow, intending to overthrow Boris and place on the throne a young man who claimed to be Dmitry, the last son of Ivan the Terrible. Before this came to pass, Boris Godunov died. The boyars accepted the pretender, doubtless believing that they could now regain some of the power they had lost under Ivan and Boris.

The 'First Dmitry', as he came to be called, reigned less than a year before he was overthrown and murdered by a mob led by the boyar Vassily (Basil) Shuisky in May 1606. By then Russia was in turmoil and Shuisky, who had been proclaimed tsar, was faced by several uprisings, one led by another pretender, the 'Second Dmitry', who again enjoyed Polish military support. The beleaguered Shuisky was obliged to ask for help from Charles IX of Sweden, an act which led King Sigismund III of Poland to declare war on Russia. In 1610, Shuisky was deposed by a Moscow assembly, and the Poles entered the capital, placing Wladislaw, King Sigismund's son, on the throne. A national uprising soon followed, led by Kuzma Minin, a meat merchant, and Prince Pozharsky. (Both are commemorated by a statue on Red Square in Moscow.) For twenty-two months the Kremlin was in a state of siege before the Poles were forced by starvation to submit.

To solve the problem of a ruler, the newly-elected *Zemski sobor*, a council of boyars, clergy, representatives of the gentry and merchants, and Cossacks, chose sixteen-year-old Michael (Mikhail) Romanov, a relative of Ivan the Terrible's popular first wife, Anastasia. Finally, the 'Time of Troubles' had come to an end.

The Early Romanovs

During the reign of Michael Romanov, stability was restored to the war-ravaged and lawless land. The Tsar, in fact, shared power with his father, Metropolitan Philaret, a nobleman experienced in state affairs, who had been a rival of Boris Godunov and had subsequently made a career in the Church. Its population decimated by warfare and starvation, Russia was in no condition to pursue an aggressive foreign policy and peace was made with Poland and Sweden. As a precaution against Tatar invasions, Michael founded fortified towns on his southern frontiers.

When not engaged in affairs of state, the Tsar indulged his passion for clocks, spending hours contemplating the timepieces sent to him as a goodwill gesture by King Gustavus Adolphus of Sweden. He subsequently ordered 200 more clocks from abroad to decorate the Kremlin, and reputedly started wearing at least three watches on his wrist on ceremonial occasions, a fashion copied by his boyars. On the day of his death in 1645, he had gone to visit his favourite place, the clock repair shop in the Kremlin, where the German clock maker, Marcelius, was working. While quietly sitting there, he suffered a fatal heart attack.

In the eventful reign of Michael's successor, Alexius (1645-76), the country recovered its strength so rapidly that the Tsar was tempted to put forward claims to Livonia, Lithuania and Little Russia (i.e. the Ukraine). Not all of these pretensions were achieved, but great progress was made towards the absorption of the Ukraine, a wilderness inhabited by the freedom-loving Cossacks and ruled since the thirteenth century by Poland and Lithuania. Russia acquired half the Ukraine, including the city of Kiev, by the Treaty of Andrussovo in 1667, after Alexius had aided the Cossack leader, Bogdan Khelmnitsky, in his fight against the Poles. The other half remained in Polish hands until 1793, when it, too, was incorporated into the Russian Empire.

An event of major importance in Alexius's reign was the *raskol* or schism which divided and weakened the Russian Orthodox Church. Until the beginning of the seventeenth century Russia had observed the Byzantine tradition that in all matters outside the sphere of dogma the ecclesiastical was subordinate to the civil power; but these traditional concepts had been to some extent undermined during the reign of Michael, when the head of the Russian Church was raised from the rank of metropolitan to patriarch, and Patriarch Philaret governed on an equal footing with his son. His immediate successors made no pretensions to such an exalted position, but when the ambitious Nikon, who had arrived in Moscow 'all humble bows and hellos', in the words of Avvakum, his contemporary, was installed as the new patriarch, he took Philaret as his model and propounded the doctrine that the spiritual is higher than the temporal power.

At first, the tall monk awed Alexius, a devoutly religious man, with his imposing physical presence and spiritual intensity, but his ambitions at last exhausted the Tsar's patience and he was formally deposed and retired to a monastery. But this was not before he had introduced a number of

St Petersburg in 1856: statue of Peter the Great in Admiralty Square.

151

112. When Peter I resolved to build a new city on the Gulf of Finland, the first major building, raised on a marshy island, was the Peter Paul Fortress. The Baroque cathedral dedicated to SS Peter and Paul with its graceful spire, the first example in Russian architecture, was built within the fortress (1712-33) by Peter's chief architect, Trezzini. From Peter's time on, all but two of the tsars were interred here.

ecclesiastical reforms to bring the Russian Church more in line with the Greek. Nikon's reforms were violently opposed by many who regarded his work as satanic. His greatest critic was the Archpriest Avvakum (1620-82), a fundamentalist passionately opposed to any change in the traditional Russian forms of worship. He argued that, while Byzantium had fallen to the Turks, Russia had preserved its faith in pristine form and to tamper with it would be sinful. Avvakum and his supporters, who came to be called Old Believers, were mercilessly persecuted. Many fled to the Far North, Siberia and the Caucasus. Rumours spread that the end of the world was approaching and several communities of Old Believers committed mass suicide, immolating themselves by setting fire to their wooden churches: like water, flames were considered to purify and such a death was seen as a way of expiating sin. 'The Old Believers,' wrote Alexander Solzhenitzyn in his masterpiece *The Gulag Archipelago*, 'eternally persecuted, eternal exiles, ...divined the ruthlessness at the heart of Authority'.

One of the effects of the schism was to weaken the Church, from which there were widespread defections, especially among the peasantry, and make it more dependent on the state. It also increased religious awareness, forcing people to make a commitment to either the official church teachings or those of the dissenters.

There was still much social unrest in the country. In 1670 Stenka Razin, a Don Cossack, led a motley army against the boyars in protest against the brutalities of serfdom. Razin's first raids were in the lower Volga region and the shores of the Caspian Sea. Then he turned northwards, winning over tens of thousands of serfs and also many peoples resentful of Muscovite rule — Bashkirs, Kalmyks and Mordvinians. The movement spread throughout the Volga region and as far north as the River Oka. For a while the insurrection posed a threat to Moscow itself, but eventually it lost momentum and was crushed by the superior military strength of the Tsar's troops. Razin was captured and executed on Red Square in 1671.

Another development of the later seventeenth century was the growth of western influence on Muscovite society, and the beginning of criticism of the old, backward ways. A prosperous foreign quarter grew up outside the capital, housing a community of fortune-seeking foreigners whose knowledge and technical skills were much needed: military men, merchants, teachers, artisans, doctors, midwives, paper manufacturers, glass-workers and others. The first stage play in Muscovy, lasting ten hours, was performed there in October 1672, and it was not long before the Kremlin itself was the scene of theatrical performances. But it was Alexius's successor, Peter the Great, who would go down in history for having violently rejected the Muscovite past and enthusiastically 'westernized' Russia.

Alexius had been twice married and when he died in 1676 left several children by each of his wives. A struggle for power ensued between the two rival families. The late tsar's eldest son, Fedor, was weak in health and died without male issue after an uneventful reign of six years (1676-82). The next in the order of succession, the weak-minded Ivan, was not suited to govern, and so the third son, Peter, born of the second marriage, was proclaimed co-tsar. As he was under age, however, his half-sister, Sophia Alexeyevna, ruled as regent in autocratic fashion for seven years. Reluctant to relinquish power, in 1689, when Peter was seventeen, she plotted to have him murdered. Forewarned of this, Peter escaped to Sergievo (Zagorsk) where nobles and troops loyal to him gathered and marched on Moscow. Having crushed all resistance, Peter confined Sophia to the Novodevichy Convent and took over the reins of government.

113. The Winter Palace in St Petersburg (overleaf) was one of several lavish new residences commissioned by Peter the Great's daughter, the Empress Elizabeth, in the mid-eighteenth century. Designed by her Italian architect, Rastrelli, in the exuburant Baroque style that she favoured, it was the fourth palace on the site. Like the Louvre, the royal residence eventually became a world-famous museum: the Hermitage.

114. St Petersburg was founded in 1703 on the delta of the Neva River where it flows into the Gulf of Finland, forming a number of islands. On this territory captured from the Swedes, Peter the Great determined to build a new capital that would be Russia's 'Window on the West', an outlet on the Baltic. Under his energetic supervision and with ruthless use of forced labour, by 1712 the construction of the new city was advanced enough for him to move his court here from Moscow.

115, 116. 'The Venice of the North', St Petersburg is crisscrossed by waterways, spanned by numerous bridges. The two sphinxes (opposite) are by the Egyptian Bridge, and the golden-winged gryphons (right) beside the attractive Bank Bridge, one of six suspension bridges built across the Griboyedev Canal in the early nineteenth century.

117. The Narva Gate, surmounted by a statue of Victory, marks the old boundary of St Petersburg: from here the road led to Narva and Revel (Tallinn). Originally a wooden structure, raised in 1814 to commemorate the bravery of the Russian Guards in the Napoleonic Wars, the triumphal arch was built in its present form, brick covered with copper sheeting, in the 1830s. The statues at the base are of ancient Russian heroes.

118. Michael Palace was built in 1825 for Alexander I's brother, the Grand Duke Michael. Its architect, Carlo Rossi, also designed the grand Square of the Arts (formerly Mikhailovsky) which it faces and the surrounding buildings and streets — a magificent piece of urban planning. Since 1895 the palace has housed the National Museum of Russian Art with a collection of over 300,000 works.

119. St Isaac's Cathedral, converted into a museum in 1931, presides over St Petersburg by virtue of its monumental scale: its dome with the lantern is over 300 ft in height; the columns of the façade each weigh 114 tons. Designed by a Frenchman, Montferrand, it was begun in 1818 and took forty years to complete. The interior is lavishly decorated with precious stones, gold, malachite and porphyry.

120. Triumphal Arch linking two wings of the huge building of the Ministry of War on Palace Square, commissioned from the Italian architect, Carlo Rossi, by Alexander I in the 1820s to mark Russia's victory over Napoleon.

121. The cathedral of the New Maidens Resurrection Convent (Voskresensky Novodevichy) at Smolny, built for Empress Elizabeth by the architect Rastrelli in luxuriant rococo style in the mid-eighteenth century. The site on the bank of the Neva was formerly occupied by tar-yards making pitch (smola) for the ship-building yards nearby, so that this fairy-tale complex, usually called Smolny Convent, goes by the inappropriate name of 'tarry'.

122. The Great Palace, also known as Catherine's Palace, at Pushkin, formerly Tsarskoye Selo ('imperial village'), 15 mi. south of St Petersburg. Originally it was a modest hunting lodge built around 1720 by Peter the Great's wife, Catherine. Her daughter, Empress Elizabeth, employed Rastrelli to transform it into a sumptuous palace with a garden façade over 300 yards long.

123. One of the main gateways of the Catherine Palace.

124. The interior of the
Catherine Palace at
Tsarskoye Selo is no less
lavishly adorned than
the façade and served
Elizabeth as a fit setting
for her extravagant
entertainments. Like the
rest of the palace, the
grand staircase with its
gilded ornamentation
was faithfully restored at
tremendous expense
after suffering almost
complete destruction in
World War II.

125. Interior of the Russian Museum, formerly the Michael Palace. When it ceased to be a grand-ducal residence, it was turned into apartments and was becoming run down before the authorities decided to make it a museum, opened by Nicholas II in 1895. Of the original interior decor, only the staircase and White Hall survived these alterations.

126, 127. The Church of the Saviour on the Blood was raised on the spot where Alexander II, the 'Tsar Liberator', was assassinated in 1881. Its silhouette, reminiscent of St Basil's in Moscow, is in striking contrast to the classical buildings around it. It is an example of the 'Russian style' favoured at the end of the nineteenth century which revived features of early national architecture.

IMPERIAL RUSSIA

Peter the Great

128. The Rostral Columns on Strelka Point on Vasilievsky Island were erected in 1810 as lighthouses to guide ships as they entered St Petersburg. The columns are decorated with symbolic ship's prows and figures representing the rivers Neva, Volga, Dnieper and Volkhov. Now the flames are lit only on festive occasions.

Peter I was a giant among his contemporaries in every sense of the word. Standing six foot six tall, powerfully built and possessing extraordinary strength, he could roll up a silver plate and walked with such huge, rapid strides that his companions had to run to keep up with him. He was, in the words of the nineteenth-century Russian writer, Alexander Herzen, 'a semi-barbarian in appearance and spirit, but a man of genius...'

One of the few surviving regimental flags from the year 1700 shows an allegory of Russia as a rowing boat, with Peter at the oars, being guided by Saturn, the ruler of the world. The image was appropriate, for ever since his childhood days, when he had repaired and learnt to handle a sailing boat he had come across by chance, Peter had had a passion for navigation. Later he was to say that if he were not the ruler of Russia, he would like to have been an English admiral. Acknowledged as the founder of the Russian Navy, Peter first started to develop the Russian fleet in 1695 in order to capture from Turkey the fortress town of Azov and gain access to the Black Sea.

Fired by the ambition to modernize his country and raise it to the first rank of European powers, Peter set out on his 'Great Embassy to Europe', visiting Prussia, Holland, Great Britain and Vienna. For him this was, above all, an extended study trip on which he could gather new ideas and engage skilled foreigners to bring the latest western technology to Russia. His visit to Vienna in the autumn of 1698 was cut short, however, by news of a mutiny of the Guards (*Streltsy*) in Moscow. He dashed home and suppressed this revolt with extreme cruelty, personally taking a hand in the mass executions. His half-sister Sophia, the instigator of the revolt, was held under even closer detention in her convent and caused him no further trouble.

During the Great Embassy, he conceived the bold notion of a war against Sweden to win a seaport on the Baltic Sea and access to western trade. What was to become known as the Great Northern War was declared in 1700 and dragged on in fits and starts for more than twenty years. Early on, in 1703, Peter captured the Swedish fortress of Nyenschanz on the River Neva and on an island nearby designated the site of the Peter-Paul Fortress, the first building of the future city of St Petersburg. King Charles XII of Sweden fought the war against Peter and the kings of Denmark and Poland with skill and courage, but suffered a heavy defeat at Poltava in 1709, the turning point of the war. Hostilities were finally ended in 1721 by the Treaty of Nystadt, by which Russia acquired a large part of the Baltic coast, including Ingria, Karelia, Livonia, Estonia and part of Finland.

Only a year later, the tireless emperor embarked on another military campaign, this time in the south, against Persia. Within a short time the whole western seaboard of the Caspian Sea and the Persian-protected khanates of Derbend and Baku had been captured. Peter was also the first Russian ruler to dream of opening up a golden road to India: he sent an armed expedition to Khiva in Central Asia, but this was defeated and his dream was unfulfilled.

In order to maintain the huge armed forces his campaigns required — military expenditure absorbed four-fifths of Russia's revenues — Peter had to reform many of the traditional administrative, social and fiscal structures of the country. One of the first major steps was to introduce compulsory military service. Another was to replace the traditional Muscovite hierarchy of titles of the nobility with the Table of Ranks, a system closer to western models. Under the three headings of the three branches of state service (armed forces, civil service and Court) he listed fourteen categories for each, corresponding to different functions and offices. The holder of an office was entitled to the *chin* (rank) corresponding to it on the list. The American journalist John Reed observed that the system still held sway in 1917: the Petrograd streets were full of 'subdued old gentlemen in uniform...going home from work in the huge, barrack-like Ministries or Government institutions, calculating perhaps how great a mortality among their superiors would advance them to the coveted *chin* of Collegiate Assessor or Privy Councillor...'

The Tsar's reforms extended to many different fields: law, police, military discipline, the navy, commerce, the sciences, the fine arts and education. He introduced a simplified new Russian alphabet to replace the Church Slavonic script, and he himself learnt Dutch and German. He even considered introducing Dutch as the official language of state. Whether in his oak-panelled study at the Petrodvoretz Palace outside St Petersburg, leading his troops, or travelling indefatigably around his vast realm, he devoted his whole mind and energies to his mission in life: to add to his empire and to 'hack a window open on Europe'.

One tangible expression of western orientation was the city of St Petersburg, founded in 1703 as a harbour for the Russian fleet. It was built as a fortress from which to threaten the Swedes, who had beleaguered the Russians for centuries, and as the spiritual centre of the new European Russia. Given the harsh climate and marshy terrain of the Neva delta, the construction of St Petersburg, undertaken at great speed, caused untold human misery. At any one time, 40,000 peasants were engaged in the building of Russia's new capital; many met an anonymous end in the marshlands or succumbed to disease and malnutrition. Losses were met simply, by drafting in fresh peasant recruits.

The Tsar was furious with any opponents of change. On his return from Europe, one of his first acts, much resented, was personally to cut off the long beards of the boyars and oblige them to wear western-style dress. One of his main targets was the Orthodox Church, whose power he considerably reduced. The clergy, for their part, saw an evil power in Peter's foreign appearance, his bulging eyes and alarming long moustaches, and called him 'the crocodile'. They had, indeed, strongly disapproved of him ever since his decree taxing beards. For Orthodox Russians, the beard was a fundamental symbol of religious belief and self-respect, and to shave was tantamount to defacing the image of man created by God.

Peter the Great's rule had been so harsh, his reign so full of radical changes, that long after his death in 1725, at the age of fifty-two, he remained a dominant figure in the minds of the people, overshadowing his successors throughout the eighteenth century, even Catherine the Great. It was she who commissioned the most famous monument to him, the Bronze Horseman, the enigmatic subject of Pushkin's poem of the same name. Designed by the French sculptor, Etienne Maurice Falconet, it was unveiled in St Petersburg in 1782 amid great pomp and ceremony.

Peter's Heirs

After Peter's death, the problem of succession arose once more. His first son, Alexius (Alexei), had died in prison, accused of treason, and his second son, Peter, by a second marriage, had died as a child. Of male heirs there remained only his grandson, another Peter, son of the ill-fated Alexius, but he was too young to rule. With the help of the Imperial Guards and Prince Menshikov, a long-time favourite of the late tsar, Peter's widow, Catherine, ascended the throne. Before extravagant living sent Catherine I to her grave only two years later, she named as her heir Peter the Great's eleven-year-old grandson. But Peter II's reign was also very brief: he died of smallpox in 1730. To avert a crisis, Peter the Great's niece, Anna, was invited to take the throne. Since her marriage to the Duke of Kurland, a small principality in the southern part of present-day Latvia, she had been living outside Russia. Now she was widowed, and decided to return to St Petersburg.

Anna's ten-year reign (1730-1740) was a period of methodical administration, during which she relied on three German advisors, her favourite courtiers: Counts von Biron, Ostermann and Munnich. Having no son, she chose as her successor her infant great-nephew, who was duly proclaimed emperor at her death, under the name of Ivan VI. However, in little more than a year, he was dethroned by the regiment of the Preobrazhenski Guards in St Petersburg, who proclaimed Princess Elizabeth, Peter the Great's daughter, Empress of All Russia.

Few daughters have made so much of the memory of their fathers as Elizabeth, whose prestige was definitely enhanced by her Petrine connection: Peter's achievements as the great 'Enlightener of Russia' were glorified at her coronation and afterwards in a wide variety of writings, odes and public orations. But Elizabeth, herself, was a magnificent figure, described by her successor, Catherine the Great, as wearing 'silvery moiré with golden braid...a black feather erect at the side of her head and many diamonds in her hair'. She was a large woman with large appetites, fond of handsome young men and fine clothes — her wardrobe is said to have contained 15,000 dresses.

Empress Elizabeth, engraving by E.P. Chemesov, 1761.

Under Elizabeth, St Petersburg established itself as the centre of government, and began to grow into a great European city. In particular, the Empress's affection for France meant that French manners and fashions gained in popularity among the Russian aristocracy. Her love of colour, extravagance and luxury is reflected in the buildings she commissioned. She invited the Italian architect, Bartolomeo Rastrelli, to build a number of palaces to impress foreign dignitaries. Among his creations, the Winter Palace, the Anitchkov Palace and the Smolny Convent stand as some of the most prodigious, perhaps excessive, examples of baroque architecture in the world. Rastrelli paid particular attention to the construction of the Catherine Palace (named after Elizabeth's mother) at Tsarskoye Selo on the outskirts of the city, where his brief was to 'transform Tsarskoye Selo into a Russian Versailles'.

During Elizabeth's reign, Russia began to play a more active role on the European stage. In the Seven Years War, which broke out when Frederick II 'the Great' of Prussia invaded Saxony in August 1756, Russia intervened on the side of Austria and France, going so far as to invade part of east Prussia and occupy Berlin in 1760. Taken aback by the Russian show of strength, Frederick wrote that it would be better to cultivate the friendship of 'these barbarians'.

When Elizabeth died in 1761, she was succeeded by her German nephew, the Duke of Holstein, who was crowned as Peter III. He quickly made himself unpopular by his undisguised aversion to everything in his adopted country and his adulation of Frederick the Great, with whom he immediately made peace on terms favourable to the almost defeated Prussian ruler. Not surprisingly, within a year of his accession he was deposed in a coup by the Imperial Guards plotted by his forceful, intelligent, German wife, and murdered shortly after. The former Princess Sophia Augusta of Anhalt-Zerbt now ascended the Russian throne as Catherine II.

Catherine the Great

Initially without strong personal standing or support, Catherine proceeded to rule for no less than thirty-four years, helped by some of her many lovers, most notably Prince Potemkin, and other long-serving ministers. During her reign Russia's territory was greatly extended: southwards, at the expense of Turkey, in the Black Sea and Caucasus regions; and, by the partitions of Poland in 1772 and 1793, south-westwards over the Ukraine and Belorussia. Towards the end of her life, the Empress became obsessed with the idea of taking Constantinople and creating a new Byzantine Empire in the Balkans, but this was never realized. Another plan, the Eastern Project, was to strike through Persia to India. In 1783 the Treaty of Protection made with the kingdom of Georgia, to defend it against the Turks and Persians, effectively turned it into a vassal state.

At home, the Empress rose early, lit her fire and made her black coffee before busily consulting some of the finest philosophers of the day on the best way to rule her vast empire. Most of all she was drawn to the French philosophers: Voltaire, Montesquieu, D'Alembert and Diderot. French became the language of the Court. Catherine published the fruits of her reading and study in the famous *Nakaz* or Great Instruction in 1767, which she presented to a Legislative Commission, comprising a broad range of deputies, who had been assembled to draft a new code of laws. However, the Instruction, an immense document with 22 chapters and more than 50 articles reflecting on political, judicial, social and economic issues, clearly showed that Catherine was in no doubt that autocratic rule was the only form of government suitable for Russia.

Catherine's reign, though eminently successful in the field of foreign affairs, was marked by frequent riots and revolts. The most serious of these was in 1773, when the Don Cossack, Emelyan Pugachev, giving himself out to be the miraculously-saved Peter III, led a great rebellion, supported mainly by Cossacks and the non-Russian Bashkirs. It took two years and all Catherine's forces to suppress the uprising and capture Pugachev, who was publicly executed in Moscow in 1775. One result was the reform of local government to centralize control and ensure a more effective system of internal security.

The rebel leader Emelyan Pugachev, engraving, 1775.

At the beginning of her reign, Catherine had given the impression of being a somewhat less arbitrary ruler than her predecessors (although she was perfectly clear of the need for an absolute ruler in Russia). She had corresponded with the most enlightened French philosophers and entertained advanced ideas of reform. But the French Revolution changed her domestic policy in the last years of her life. In the first serious cases of intellectual persecution of her reign, she exiled the serf-owner Alexander Radischev to Siberia for his book, influenced by Rousseau, criticizing serfdom. This was followed in 1792 by the arrest of Nikolai Novikov, a Freemason who had been a pioneer of education and enlightened charity.

The Empress was, however, in her declining years. The splendour of her Court was fading. Seven years after news of the French Revolution had seized St Petersburg with panic, Catherine died from a stroke in November 1796, to be succeeded by her only son, Paul.

From Paul I to Nicholas I

Paul I had always hated his mother, believing her guilty of his father's murder (though rumour had it that he was the son of one of Catherine's lovers). Disliking the Winter Palace, where she had lived, he decided to build himself a new residence, the Michael Castle. Since he lived in constant fear of assassination, it was designed for maximum security. He furnished the castle by stripping the magnificent Tauride Palace that Catherine had built for her lover, Potemkin, and taken over after his death. The latter building was given to the Horse Guards for use as barracks. Habitually dressed in a plain green uniform, great-boots and a large hat, he was notoriously fond of military drill and applied military methods to his government, thereby quickly alienating his ministers and the nobles at court. He replaced the army's old uniforms with uncomfortable new ones in the Prussian style; he reintroduced corporal punishment for the nobility; he prohibited the wearing of round hats: the numerous decrees were bewildering and often capricious, reflecting his unstable, despotic character.

In foreign affairs, Russia became involved in the Napoleonic Wars. Alarmed by the extent of France's conquests, Paul dispatched an army under General Suvurov to help the Austrians in northern Italy, but in 1801 he decided to withdraw it and resume relations with France. He, too, embarked on a project to conquer India, but the mission was a total failure. Eventually, his domestic and foreign policies proved so contradictory that a group of officers, almost certainly with the connivance of his heir, Alexander, decided to eliminate him. Five years after his coronation, he was assassinated in the middle of the night in his new, 'top-security' Michael Castle in St Petersburg.

All hopes of progress were now pinned on the twenty-four-year-old Alexander I, who appeared at first to be a reforming tsar. He had even insisted he would abdicate once he had established an enlightened government. The early part of his reign was a period of generous ideas and reforms: the rehabilitation of over 12,000 people banished or dismissed from their posts by his father; the prohibition of torture as a means of criminal investigation; the lifting of the ban on foreign books and travel; and the investigation of the possibility of a new constitution. This task was entrusted to Speransky, the son of a village priest, who had made a brilliant career in the civil service. But although Speransky proposed an excellent new Statute of State Laws, it was never adopted, and he was dismissed from his post in 1812.

On the foreign front, Russia was entering a new phase in its history. Under Paul, it had formally annexed Georgia, at that time under threat from Persia. Now it aspired to exercise a dominant influence on European affairs. In 1805 Russia re-entered the war against Napoleon, but after defeats at Austerlitz and elsewhere, Alexander withdrew from the allied coalition and in 1807 formed an alliance with France, sealed by the Treaty of Tilsit. This alliance was broken five years later when Napoleon invaded Russia. Three months later, following the bloody battle of Borodino, he entered Moscow, only to find it abandoned. Shortly after, the city was consumed by fire and the French, short of supplies, with no government to negotiate with and faced by the onset of winter, had no alternative but to turn homewards. The story of the retreat from Moscow is well-known. Of the French Grand Army, 600,000 strong, less than a tenth survived the Russian campaign. Many died at the disastrous crossing of the River Berezina in Belorussia, many others from disease, hunger and cold. In 1814 the Russian army, led by Alexander, triumphantly entered Paris.

After the Napoleonic Wars, Alexander's liberalism dwindled. With the conclusion of peace in Europe, he had achieved the prominent position in European politics which had long been his ambition. Firmly believing he had been chosen by Providence to secure the happiness of the European nations, he spent long periods abroad, negotiating a Holy Alliance, based on Christian principles, with the other great powers. One of the first results of this was that Russia, Prussia and Austria split up among themselves what little was left of Poland. In his absence abroad, he left the administration to his unpopular chief adviser, the brutal Count A. A. Arakcheyev.

Returning home, the liberal-minded young Russian officers who had spent several years in western Europe during the Napoleonic Wars, were disappointed to find the autocracy unchanged and the peasants, who had fought side by side with their masters during the war, still enslaved as serfs. Disillusioned, they became convinced of the need for social and political reform, a conviction reinforced by the harsh Arakcheyev regime.

In September 1825 Alexander went to join his wife, Elizabeth, who was convalescing in Taganrog on the Sea of Azov. Two months after his arrival, his death was announced, shortly to be followed by that of Elizabeth. There seems to have been something mysterious about his death and later a rumour spread that he was living as a hermit in a monastery in Western Siberia. Since Alexander had no direct heir, the throne should rightly have passed to his brother Constantine, but he had previously renounced the succession in favour of his younger brother, Nicholas. However, this fact was not generally known, so there was considerable confusion and also widespread dissatisfaction, since Constantine was considered to be less reactionary than Nicholas. A group of liberally-minded aristocratic officers, inspired by the ideas of the French Revolution and plotting constitutional reform, decided that this was the moment to take action.

Nicholas's reign began tragically. On 14 December (Old Style) 1825, the day the armed forces were due to swear allegiance to the new ruler in Senate Square, some 3,000 troops, incited by their officers, refused to take the oath and called for Constantine to be tsar. They were eventually surrounded and outnumbered, however, by troops loyal to Nicholas. By evening they had been scattered and dispersed, but not before the snow-covered square was drenched in blood. The Military Governor of St Petersburg and spectators had been killed, as well as many soldiers. Five of the Decembrists, as the conspirators were called, were executed, the rest were sentenced to terms of hard labour, exiled to Siberia or reduced to the ranks for life. Other rebellions in the Ukraine were also suppressed.

The Decembrist revolt convinced the reactionary Nicholas that Russia must be ruled with a firm hand or else there would be more revolution. Government control was tightened by the establishment of the Corps of Gendarmes, political police organized on military lines who operated throughout the county. Severe press censorship was introduced to prevent revolutionary ideas from germinating. Russians were again forbidden to travel abroad and it was made difficult for foreigners to gain access to the country. In response, there emerged a new phenomenon, the intelligentsia, thinking Russians with no place in government, who voiced increasingly bitter criticism of the autocratic regime, with its serfdom and harsh army discipline. Despite the police repression, by the 1840s groups of anarchists, followers of the French philosopher, Prudhoń, and the Russian, Bakunin, were meeting secretly in St Petersburg, Moscow and some other cities.

In foreign policy, Nicholas was a determined empire-builder. Within a few years of his accession, Russia gained a part of Persian Armenia with its Christian population and the city of Erevan, and won a victory against the Turks. In 1831 the Polish revolt provoked a crisis, but was suppressed. In 1849 Russia intervened in Hungary. The systematic conquest of the Caucasus, one of the longest and most draining campaigns in Russian military history, was undertaken. It may have contributed largely to Russia's defeat in the Crimean War, which broke out in 1854 as a result of Russian attempts to protect the rights and privileges of the Orthodox communities in Turkey. Alarmed by Russian expansion, Britain and France came to Turkey's aid and Austria, too, joined the coalition of Russia's enemies. However, before the war was concluded, Nicholas died in March 1855. It remained for his son, Alexander II, to agree to humiliating peace terms at the Congress of Paris, whereby Russia lost its right to send its Black Sea fleet into the Mediterranean.

Nicholas I, Emperor of All the Russias

The Tsar Liberator

The Crimean War proved to be one of the greatest catalysts of reform in Russia. Just as peace was being concluded in Paris, the new ruler called together his marshals and announced that it would be 'better to abolish serfdom from above than to wait until the serfs begin to liberate themselves from below'. Thus, Alexander II embarked on a series of domestic reforms that earned him the title of 'Liberator'.

The question of serfdom had been raised long before, in the reign of Catherine the Great. Even Nicholas I had been in favour of its abolition, although nothing had been done about it. In 1861 the serfs were finally emancipated. All were given personal freedom together with allotments of land, the previous owners being recompensed by the state with treasury bonds. The peasants were to repay the bonds to the state over a forty-nine-year period. To the village commune (*mir*) was given the task of distributing the land. Over sixty years later, the eighty-year-old Secretary of State, Koulomzin, who had taken an active part in the emancipation, thought the original idea had been a mistake. He told the French ambassador that the conveyance of the land to the *mir* had imbued the Russian peasant with the communistic notion that the land belongs to those who cultivate it, and not to a private owner. Two years before the 1917 Revolution, he concluded that the whole future of Russia depended on the peasant being given personal ownership of land, and hoped (in vain) that in fifteen or twenty years the system of private property would have completely ousted that of communal ownership among the peasantry.

At the time, the emancipation of the serfs raised hopes of further political and social changes. Concern about Russia's future had given rise to a notable debate between the Westerners and Slavophiles. While the former blamed Russia's backwardness on its eastern connections and looked to the West for enlightenment, the latter, hating western materialism, sought salvation in Russia's ancient culture, with its medieval peasant commune and its religious roots. One of the main strands of thinking in the 1870s was *narodnichestvo* or populism, based on the belief that a socialist revolution was needed to overthrow the existing order. The possibility of revolution in Russia had been considered by Marx and Engels, especially after 1868 when Marx learnt, to his surprise, that a translation of *Das Kapital* was being printed in St Petersburg. The chief Russian revolutionaries, Bakunin and Lavrov, called on young people to abandon their university studies in order to encourage the peasants to revolt. Thousands of idealistic students went into the countryside, but many were disillusioned when the peasants either ignored them or turned them over to the constabulary.

As their hopes of change were frustrated, the revolutionaries decided there was a need for a disciplined party which might use acts of violence as a weapon to achieve reforms. A number of prominent officials were accordingly condemned to death by secret terrorist tribunals and in some cases the sentences were carried out. The wave of terrorism culminated in the assassination of Alexander II by four terrorists on the Ekaterinsky Embankment in St Petersburg in 1881. (The Church of Christ Resurrected was later built on the spot where the Tsar was mortally wounded.) Ironically, the Tsar Liberator had been on the point of initiating changes leading to constitutional reform.

The outbreak of terrorism only served to intensify political repression. Taking the advice of his 'Grand Inquisitor', Pobedonostsev, the conservative Alexander III who now came to the throne severely punished all revolutionaries and further increased the power of the police. More and more anarchist, populist and socialist revolutionaries were dispatched to Siberia. Thanks to such tight security, Alexander III escaped the violent end met by his father and by his son, Nicholas II, who succeeded him in 1894.

129. Cathedral of St Dmitry in Vladimir, built in limestone in the twelfth century in the distinctive style of architecture that evolved in Vladimir and Suzdal. Previously, Russian churches were of wood, but at this time the Byzantine manner of building in stone and brick was adopted. The upper part of the façade is covered with low-relief carvings of religious, historical and legendary figures.

*130. Church of the Intercession,
Bogolyubovo, on the outskirts of Vladimir,
one of the supreme examples of early
Russian architecture. It was built in his
native village in 1165 by Prince Andrei
Bogolyubovsky, Prince of Vladimir-Suzdal.
Andrei, son of Prince Yury Dolgoruky,
founder of Vladimir, Yaroslavl, Moscow
and other new townships, was himself a
notable warrior and builder, particularly in
and around Vladimir, his capital.*

131. Church of the Prophet Elijah (1647-50), built for the merchants of Yaroslavl, at that time a prosperous trading town on the Volga. Typical of the local architectural style, it combines the monumentality of earlier churches with complex assymetrical groupings of relatively independent structures. The interior of the church is decorated with beautiful frescoes.

179

132, 134. Cathedral of the Transfiguration (1714) and Church of the Intercession of the Virgin (1764) on Kizhi Island, Lake Onega, examples of the ancient Russian tradition of raising multi-domed wooden churches, few of which have survived.

133. Detail of the meticulously dovetailed slats of wood (shingles) used for the roofing. Legend has it that when the cathedral was finished, the master-builder threw his axe into the lake, declaring: 'Master Nestor built this church; there is not another like it, and there never will be.'

135. *Old Cathedral of the Icon of the
Virgin of the Don, the first stone church to
be built in Donskoy Monastery. Founded in
the 1590s as part of the ring of fortifications to defend Moscow from Tatar and
other attacks, the monastery also has a
much larger New Cathedral. The tiers of
small ornamental gables (kokoshniki) are
typical of Muscovite churches of the time.*

136. *Holy Trinity, the oldest church (1422)
of the revered Troitse-Sergiev Monastery at
Sergiev Posad (formerly Zagorsk). The
interior was decorated by the greatest of
early Russian painters, Andrei Rublev.*

137. *Troitse-Sergiev Monastery and the town of Sergiev Posad (Zagorsk), some 40 mi. north-east of Moscow. The monastery (lavra) was founded in the fourteenth century by St Sergei of Radonezh, the 'peasant saint' of Russia, who in 1380 united the Russian princes against the Tatars at the battle of Kulikovo.*

138. *New Jerusalem Monastery at Istra in the Moscow region, built in 1656 and remodelled in the eighteenth century, is an original and grand example of the 'tent church' architectural style popular in this period. It owes its existence to the energetic Patriarch Nikon, whose reforms of the rites of Orthodox worship led to the break-away of the 'Old Believers' sect.*

139. Church of the Ascension in the town of Romanovo-Borisoglebsk, one of the grandest fortress towns of the 'Golden Ring' of ancient cities that surrounds Moscow. Borisoglebsk, named after the first two Russian saints, Boris and Gleb, originated as a fortress in the middle of the sixteenth century.

140. Savvino-Storozhevsky Monastery, on a hill overlooking the Moskva River, a mile or so from the ancient town of Zvenigorod, first chronicled in 1328. The monastery itself was founded in 1389 under Prince Yury Zvenigorodsky, whose confessor, Savva, was the first abbot.

141. Church of the Archangel Michael in the Andronikov Monastery of the Saviour, built in a restrained version of the Moscow Baroque style. The fortified monastery now houses the Andrei Rublev Icon Museum.

142. *Novodevichy (New Maidens) Convent,*
on a bend in the Moskva River, has some
fine examples of sixteenth- and seven-
teenth-century architecture: Smolensk
Cathedral (left), the bell-tower (centre) and
the Church of the Transfiguration (right).

143. *Monastery of St James beside Lake Nero, a mile or so west of Rostov Veliky (Rostov the Great), one of Russia's oldest cities. First mentioned in chronicles in 826, in the eleventh and twelfth centuries it was the capital of a principality.*

144. Church of the Saviour-on-Gorodok at Zvenigorod in the Moscow region. This beautiful stone edifice was built in 1400 on top of the earth fortifications called Gorodok rising above the Moskva River.

REVOLUTION
AND
COMMUNISM

On the Eve

The early reign of Nicholas II was a period of rapid industrial and agricultural development, and even of hopeful political change. Between 1900 and 1913, industrial output rose by 62 per cent, Russian farm produce and raw materials were exported to the West, and foreign investment was encouraged by promises of high dividends and subsidies. French, German, British and Belgian investors all acquired interests in Russia. Agricultural productivity rose rapidly as a result of agrarian reforms introduced by Prime Minister Peter Stolypin between 1906 and 1911.

Calls for reform of Russian political life were growing, supported by the *zemstvos*, representatives of local self-governing districts. But when their proposals for civil rights, freedom of speech, assembly, the press and conscience, equality before the law, and a parliamentary system of government, were rejected, the rift between the government bureaucracy and the professional classes and aristocracy widened.

One major cause of discontent was the war with Japan, begun early in 1904 as the result of a dispute over Manchuria. Military triumphs might have boosted the imperial government and provided some distraction, but the news from the front was of humiliating defeats. The sinking of the entire Russian fleet in the straits of Tsushima in May 1905 sent shock waves back to the capital, where there was already considerable unrest. Factory workers, encouraged by clandestine revolutionaries, were mounting protests against their appalling working conditions. Strikes were numerous and in 1905 reached such a peak that they came close to full-scale revolution.

On 22 January 1905, a day that came to be known as Bloody Sunday, a priest called Father Gapon led a great crowd of people in a peaceful protest march through the snowy streets of St Petersburg towards the Winter Palace, bearing a petition to Nicholas II listing their grievances and requests. Instead of the expected audience with the Tsar, the petitioners met with troops and police bullets that killed scores and wounded hundreds more. Bloody Sunday was the spark that ignited the revolution of 1905. Besides arousing immense public anger, it set off a tremendous wave of strikes throughout the country, involving nearly half a million people. One incident in June, the dramatic mutiny of the sailors of the Battleship *Potemkin*, was the inspiration for Eisenstein's famous film of that name.

Before the end of the year the tsarist government had capitulated. Nicholas II issued the celebrated October Manifesto, drafted by the experienced statesman, Count Witte, who had earned respect during the negotiations following Russia's defeat in the war with Japan. In this the Tsar expressed his 'great and heavy grief' at the rioting and disturbances, granted his subjects 'personal inviolability, freedom of conscience, speech, assembly and association', and promised parliamentary government through an elected national assembly or *Duma*.

Though not everyone believed Nicholas — contemporary cartoons depicted him as a crocodile shedding tears — the concessions triggered political ferment. Several new parties appeared: the Bolsheviks and Mensheviks, two factions of the Social Democratic Party, who subscribed to extreme left-wing ideas; the more moderate Constitutional Democrats (Cadets) and Octobrists; and the Monarchists, supporting the Tsar. There were also Finnish, Polish and Ukrainian national parties.

However, the parliamentary experiment was short-lived. The first Duma, in which over 40 parties were represented, with the moderate Cadets in control, made the first and last attempt to gain something from the 1905 revolution. But its proposal to pass land-law reforms damaging to the conservative nobility prompted the obdurate Nicholas II to exercise his prerogative to dismiss the assembly. From 1907 onwards, the second, third and

145. Typical of old Russia are these trading or market lanes in the centre of Kostroma, one of the most beautiful of the country's historic cities. Situated on the Volga, it has a magnificent skyline created by its medieval monasteries, cathedrals and parish churches.

fourth Dumas has less power and were incapable of tackling Russia's mounting problems.

On 28 June 1914, the heir-presumptive to the Austro-Hungarian throne, Archduke Francis Ferdinand, and his wife were assassinated while on a visit to Sarajevo, an act that triggered off the First World War. Russia entered on the side of France and Britain against Austria and Germany. At first the war inspired an extraordinary wave of patriotism, reminiscent of 1812, but by the third year the Russian people had suffered terrible casualties and deprivation. Out of 13 million men mobilized in three years, two million were dead, while shortage of food supplies at home was resulting in widespread starvation.

Matters were not helped by the Tsar's indecisiveness and the fact that his unpopular German wife, Alexandra, had fallen under the influence of the licentious Rasputin. The monk's apparent ability to control the bleeding of the haemophiliac tsarevich led her to seek his advice on all matters, state as well as family, and tolerate his scandalous behaviour. Recent research suggests, though, that the myth of the 'mad monk' is untrue. Rasputin was undoubtedly a drunk and a lecher, but far from having a malign political influence, during the First World War, which he predicted would be a blood bath, his advice was ignored by the Tsar. Be that as it may, his familiar presence at Court was considered so damaging to the imperial family that in the winter of 1916 Prince Felix Yusopov and Grand Duke Dmitry plotted to get rid of Rasputin. This proved a difficult task: when cyanide poison and shooting had not finished him off, he was thrown, still breathing, under the ice of the Neva.

Disorder was, nonetheless, spreading at home and at the front, where troops were increasingly demoralized by shortage of military supplies, food and clothing, their inept leadership and the agitation for peace by revolutionaries in their ranks. In Petrograd, as St Petersburg had been renamed to

St Petersburg in 1856: Sennaia Ploschad (Haymarket).

194

make it sound more Russian, the forces of anarchy were swelling. Troops unwilling to be sent to the front joined the civilian food riots. Politicians urged the Tsar to abdicate in favour of his son, in order to save the country from revolution. Nicholas II, then at his headquarters in Mogilev and unable to reach Petrograd, abdicated on 15 March 1917, but in favour of his brother, Grand Duke Michael. A day later, Michael also renounced the throne, thereby ending three hundred years of Romanov rule.

Lenin Takes the Helm

The abdication resulted in a power vacuum: the army was at the front, the Duma carried no real weight, and the Soviet (Council) of Workers and Soldiers Deputies that had been set up during the riots lacked a strong power base. After much haggling with the Soviet, the Duma had formed a Provisional Government, in which Alexander Kerensky, a socialist lawyer, was the dominant figure. Meanwhile, the news from Russia had reached the forty-seven-year-old Vladimir Ilych Lenin, leader of the Bolsheviks, who was in exile in Switzerland. In April he travelled to Petrograd in a sealed train under the protection of Germany, which was naturally keen to see Russian military strength further undermined by chaos at home. On his arrival at the Finland Station in Petrograd, from the top of an armoured car Lenin delivered the first of a series of speeches announcing his political programme. Rejecting co-operation with the Provisional Government, he called for a socialist, proletarian revolution in Russia and world-wide, with all power to the workers' soviets, and peace, bread and freedom for the people.

In the months that followed there were continuing demonstrations in Petrograd and elsewhere, demanding an end to the war and 'All power to the soviets'. But despite the passions aroused, an attempted Bolshevik coup in July failed to dispose of the Provisional Government, now firmly under Kerensky's control. Many Bolsheviks were arrested, including Trotsky, another prominent leader, who had returned from exile in America, and Lenin went into hiding in Finland.

But the situation changed in September, when General Kornilov marched on Petrograd to attempt a counter-revolutionary coup. In order to defeat him, Kerensky was forced to ask for the help of the Petrograd Soviet. This strengthened the position of the Soviet, of which Trotsky, released from prison, now became the president.

'Conditions were daily more chaotic,' wrote the American journalist, John Reed, who was in Petrograd at the time. 'Hundreds of thousands of soldiers were deserting the front and beginning to move in vast, aimless tides over the face of the land. The peasants of the Tambov and Tver Governments, tired of waiting for land, exasperated by the repressive measures of the Government, were burning manor houses and massacring landowners. Immense strikes and lock-outs convulsed Moscow, Odessa, and the coal mines of the Don. Transport was paralysed; the army was starving, and in the big cities there was no bread.'

It was against this background that Lenin slipped back into Petrograd in disguise and established himself at the Bolshevik headquarters in the Smolny Institute. He had decided on an armed rising against the Provisional Government. On 7 November 1917, the Red Guards, organized by Trotsky, went into action, seizing key points throughout the city, storming the Winter Palace, and arresting the helpless members of the Provisional Government, though not Kerensky, who had managed to escape early in the day in a car provided by the American Embassy.

Next day, in a room thick with cigarette smoke, crowded with stern-faced soldiers and armed workers, the determined Bolsheviks announced that they had formed a new government, called the Council of People's Commissars, presided over by Lenin. Trotsky was to be commissar for foreign affairs and an active revolutionary from Georgia, J. V. Djugashvili (known to his comrades as Stalin), commissar for nationalities. Two decrees were also issued: one calling for an early peace, the second announcing the abolition of private ownership of land and its provisional transfer to the control of the peasants' soviets.

Lenin described his new government as provisional until the election of a Constituent Assembly, scheduled for 12 November. After these genuinely free elections, the Bolsheviks, as expected, were in the minority. When the Assembly turned down their radical reform programme, Bolshevik Red Guards forcibly evicted the delegates and the assembly was dissolved. This seizure of control over the government effectively put an end to prospects of parliamentary democracy in Russia. To achieve their goal, the Bolsheviks resorted to the use of terror tactics coupled with propaganda. Lenin immediately created a ruthless secret police called the *Cheka* and launched a massive propaganda programme: Bolsheviks hurried on speeding trains to the farthest ends of the country, spreading news of the revolution.

Early in 1918, the Bolsheviks renamed themselves the Communist Party and moved the capital from Petrograd, with its imperial associations, to Moscow, which was safer from foreign attack. In March, Trotsky negotiated the long-awaited, but humiliating peace of Brest-Litovsk, whereby Russia surrendered to Germany the Baltic provinces, the Ukraine, Finland, the Caucasus, Belorussia and Poland. The armistice freed front-line troops to fight for the Bolshevik cause in the civil war that had broken out in the country between the Reds and the Whites. Pressed on all sides, the Communist Government abandoned the idea of a trial for the deposed Nicholas II, under arrest with his wife, son and four daughters in the Urals. To eliminate the danger it represented, the entire imperial family was murdered in July 1918.

A centre of opposition to the Bolshevik regime was in the south, where the Cossacks of the Don joined the White Army under General Denikin. There was also resistance to Bolshevik rule in eastern Russia and the Urals, as well as in the ethnically non-Russian regions of the former empire, where attempts were made to gain independence. The White forces received considerable foreign military support in the course of 1918 and 1919 and initially won a number of victories, but by the end of 1920 the Red Army, inspired by revolutionary fervour and brilliantly organized by Trotsky, was in control almost everywhere. In the aftermath of the Civil War, over a million people emigrated.

By 1921 the country was in dire economic straits as a result of the war, revolution, civil strife, and the policy of War Communism, whereby all land, railways, ports, factories and other means of production had been taken over by the state. This had proved highly unpopular and had not solved the urgent problem of alleviating widespread famine. Faced by this critical situation, Lenin made a political *volte-face*, introducing the New Economic Policy, which made extensive concessions to private enterprise, though it was stressed at the time that this was merely a temporary expedient and there would be no permanent return to capitalism.

In December 1922 the Communist Government consolidated its victories by founding the Union of Soviet Socialist Republics (U.S.S.R.), which at that time consisted of four republics: Russia, the Ukraine, Belorussia and Transcaucasia. The Russian Federal Republic, the first to have been formed after the Bolshevik revolution, was to be the largest and most influential in the Soviet Union.

Believing the country was not ripe for the democratic process, Lenin had ensured that all power was concentrated in the hands of the Communist Party leadership, but when he died at the early age of fifty-three in January 1924, he left no clear rules of succession and the Communist Party entered a phase of fierce internal strife. Though Trotsky, the founder of the Red Army, seemed the most likely successor, his position was threatened by Josif Vissarionovich Stalin, by now the secretary general of the Party. No-one yet realised the full extent of Stalin's ruthlessness, his readiness to use force as the chief instrument for achieving his aims. In his testament, however, Lenin warned against too much power being concentrated in Stalin's hands.

Stalin's Reign of Terror

By 1927 Stalin had managed to get Trotsky expelled from the Party and exiled to Alma Ata. (Two years later he was exiled from the Soviet Union and eventually settled in Mexico, where he was murdered by a Soviet agent in 1940.) It was rapidly becoming apparent that, in the words of Nikolai Bukharin, another inner party member, Stalin 'will strangle us all'. By 1929 the wily Georgian had outmanoeuvred all his rivals to become the most powerful man in the whole of the Soviet Union and begun to implement his new socialist policy for the collectivization of agriculture. Between 1929 and 1938 more than five million peasant holdings were forcibly collectivized, causing untold suffering, particularly in the Ukraine, where resistance was fiercest, and two years of man-made famine. All over the countryside villages were invaded by Red Army troops, who set up 'committees of the poorest' required to list the names of the richer peasants (*kulaks*) in the neighbourhood. Their property was confiscated to make way for the new collective farms, and the kulaks, stripped of their possessions, were either killed on the spot as 'class enemies' or sent into exile. 'It was all very bad and difficult — but necessary,' Stalin told Winston Churchill in 1942.

Collectivization created a whole new class of dispossessed people, thus making cheap labour available for Stalin to implement his other major programme: industrialization. At terrible human cost, a number of grandiose projects were completed: the Dnieper dam in 1932; the Magnitogorsk steel plant in the Urals; the Baltic-White Sea Canal. Architects designed huge housing projects. Numerous mass sports demonstrations with disciplined columns of men and women participating in gymnastic feats glorified 'Soviet achievements'. But it was easier to build socialism than to live in the emerging totalitarian state. The repressions of the Great Terror began in 1934 with the assassination of Sergei Kirov, the Leningrad Party chief and second most powerful man in the country. In the space of two or three years the purges had decimated the elite of industry, science, the academic world, the civil service and armed forces. By 1939 at least 12 million people had been sent to their graves by the Stalinist state.

In August 1939 the Soviet Union signed a non-aggression pact with the newly powerful Nazi Germany. To Adolf Hitler, the pact gave the freedom to attack Poland, thereby starting the Second World War, and to Stalin, the opportunity of moving Soviet troops into the independent Baltic states, annexed by the Soviet Union in 1940. An unacknowledged aim of the pact was to give the Soviet Union more time to build up its armed forces in preparation for a possible future German invasion, but, despite the time gained, the Red Army was still not prepared for the German onslaught when it came in June 1941.

No-one imagined how quickly and how deeply into the country the Germans would penetrate. Ten years after the terrible programme of collectivization and at the tail end of the Great Terror, it was natural for many people to welcome the Germans as liberators from the Communist regime. By September the invading army had reached the outskirts of Leningrad. By October they were fighting for Moscow. But somehow enough troops were brought up to defend the capital. Leningrad was less fortunate: it remained under siege for 900 days during one of the worst winters, when temperatures dropped to 30 degrees C. below zero. There was no heating, no light, no transport, no food or water, while bombs and shells were falling. Not until mid-1942 was the German advance halted at Stalingrad. After a battle lasting over five months the German army was forced into retreat, and in May 1945 the war ended with the capture of Berlin by the Red Army.

The Soviet Union emerged from the war triumphant, but at a terrible cost: the total number of dead exceeded 20 million. The allied leaders met to discuss the future of 'Old Europe' at the Teheran and Yalta conferences, with the result that Stalin was given administrative control over the countries of Eastern and Central Europe, but on condition there would be free elections, allowing each country to determine its own destiny. In fact, Stalin betrayed the agreement: Communist regimes were imposed in Poland, East Germany, Czechoslovakia, Hungary, Rumania, Bulgaria and Albania, and a Communist government came to power in Yugoslavia. Western governments began to fear that the Soviet advance would overflow into Western Europe itself, and the wartime allies swiftly became antagonists in the Cold War.

In the post-war period there were hopes in the Soviet Union that once the wartime devastation had been repaired, life in the country might improve. But the terror resumed as national groups were accused of wartime treason. Ethnic Germans and Crimean Tatars were just some of the nations who were deported and forcibly resettled in the Far East and Central Asia. 'For every nation exiled,' wrote Nobel Prize winner Alexander Solzhenitzyn, 'an epic will someday be written — on its separation from its native land and its destruction in Siberia.'

With age, the leader grew more and more suspicious of the whole world, seeing potential plots and enemies everywhere. Campaigns were launched to eliminate academics, artists and writers, and anti-Semitism was encouraged. An Orwellian fear reigned. 'The darkness thickened beyond all endurance,' wrote Svetlana Alliluyeva, Stalin's daughter, about the winter of 1952-53. 'People were afraid to speak, everything grew very still as before a storm.' His death on 11 March 1953 had a traumatic impact on many millions, who had been conditioned to think of him as immortal and irreplaceable. Left in total and utter bewilderment, they mourned his death as a great tragedy. Hundreds were crushed in the stampede to see his body lying in state in the Red Square Mausoleum, where Lenin's embalmed body already lay. But many breathed a sigh of relief, as if, in Alliluyeva's words, 'the hour of freedom had struck'.

The Thaw

Stalin's death provoked a dynastic crisis. While the people, hoping for a 'Tsar Liberator', waited to see what the future might hold, inside the Kremlin, a dramatic power struggle was in progress involving Georgy Malenkov, N. A. Bulganin, Lavrenty Beria and Nikita Khrushchev. This ended in Beria's death, Malenkov's removal and the strengthening of Khruschev's position: Khrushchev became general secretary of the Party, and Bulganin, official head of state, a position from which he was later ousted. It fell to Khrushchev, 'vigorous, downright and stubborn,' in the words of British Prime Minister Anthony Eden, to wrestle with Stalin's ghost. The first round was in 1956 when he broke the silence on the Stalin years in a secret speech at the Twentieth Party Congress, attacking the Stalin cult and exposing his crimes against his political associates. The second round was in 1961 when the Twenty-second Party Conference attacked Stalin's memory again, leading to the removal of the embalmed corpse from the Red Square mausoleum to a grave in the Kremlin wall. Khrushchev's speech at the Twentieth Party Congress, though not made public at the time, nonetheless had a momentous impact. 'The ice broke and was on the move,' wrote Alliluyeva. Thousands were released from prisons and concentration camps with the official admission that they had been wrongly condemned. This was the period symbolically referred to as 'the thaw' by Ilya Ehrenburg in his novella of the same name, in which, for the first time, mention was made of the repressions.

Khrushchev promised that true Communism and general prosperity would be attained by the 1980s. But although the launching of Sputnik in October 1957 and the first manned space flight by Yury Gagarin in 1961 were manifestations of Soviet might, on the domestic level, milk, meat, fruit and other necessities were still in short supply in the shops. To improve the situation, Khrushchev launched an agricultural policy of ploughing up virgin lands in Kazakstan and Siberia which ended disastrously: in 1963 the Soviet Union, a major exporter of grain in imperial times, was humiliatingly obliged to buy Canadian wheat.

Military power proved more substantial than promises of prosperity. Soviet tanks went into Hungary in 1956 to suppress an attempt by the Hungarian government to withdraw from the Warsaw Pact. There were also repressions in Georgia; and in 1962 the world was brought to the brink of nuclear war when the Soviet Union attempted to install missiles in Cuba, but was thwarted by President Kennedy. One outcome of the Cuban missile crisis, however, was a massive build-up of the Soviet Navy under Khrushchev's

Russian artillery in action, nineteenth-century engraving.

successor, Leonid Brezhnev. In the early 1960s, a serious breach between the Soviet Union and Communist China further undermined Khrushchev's position. In autumn 1964 he was ousted by a palace coup and succeed by Leonid Brezhnev as first secretary and Alexei Kosygin as prime minister.

The Brezhnev Years

Following Khrushchev's removal, people sensed a reverse movement, a freezing up again. Brezhnev's harder line was demonstrated by the intensified persecution of political dissidents. In foreign affairs, the 'Brezhnev Doctrine' decreed that the Soviet Union had the right to suppress any deviation from Communism in satellite countries. This was put into practice when Soviet and other Warsaw Pact forces invaded Czechoslovakia in August 1968. A much less successful attempt to enforce the doctrine began in December 1979 with the invasion of Afghanistan. This decade-long war ended with the withdrawal of Soviet troops in 1988.

Although some Russians in the 1990s would look back on the stability of the Brezhnev era with nostalgia, it was a period of stagnation, when economic failures became more frequent and unresolved problems multiplied. One problem was the centralized form of government and enormous, creaking, bureaucratic apparatus that stifled initiative and encouraged waste. It was a pyramidal structure: the *nomenklatura* or ruling elite represented a tiny section of society, only 0.35 per cent of the total population in 1970. Enjoying a variety of privileges, they were satisfied with the *status quo* and opposed to any change or new ideas. Naturally enough, they clung to their positions for as long as possible: when Brezhnev died in 1982, the average age of the Politburo, the top decision-making body of the Soviet political system, was sixty-eight.

Brezhnev was succeeded by the ailing, sixty-eight-year-old Yury Andropov, who had masterminded the crushing of the Hungarian uprising in 1956 and had headed the KGB for some fifteen years. He immediately launched a campaign against corruption, but died only fourteen months later before much had been achieved. His successor, the seventy-two-year-old Konstantin Chernenko, died after only a year in office in March 1985. Finally, it was the turn of the younger generation, represented by Mikhail Gorbachev, to try and restructure the Soviet Union, which was by now clearly in a state of profound economic crisis. No-one, the new Party first secretary included, could have predicted the rapidity of future developments, leading to the dismantling of the Communist Party and the Soviet Union itself.

Perestroika

146. *The combination of architecture, choral music, colourful frescoes, icons, brightly burning candles and aromatic incense make the Russian Orthodox service an experience that gratifies the senses and uplifts the spirit. It was the beauty of the Orthodox liturgy that induced Prince Vladimir of Kiev to adopt Christianity at the end of the tenth century.*

On coming to power, Gorbachev campaigned energetically to rouse the Soviet Union from its stagnation. In February 1986 the policy of *perestroika*, 'restructuring', aimed at reorganizing the economy within the framework of Communism, was formally adopted at the Twenty-seventh Party Congress, to be followed shortly afterwards by political and cultural reforms. For the first time since the 1917 Revolution, the press was given a degree of freedom and open political debates were allowed as a result of the twin policy of *glasnost*, 'openness'. In order to expose and weed out corruption and inefficiency, the press and other mass media were encouraged to speak frankly. Once out of their straight-jacket, there was no way of constricting them again.

147. Session of the Holy Synod, the principal ecclesiastical authority of the Russian Orthodox Church, which meets every six months to administer church affairs. It is composed of permanent members: the Patriarch and the metropolitans of St Petersburg and Novgorod, and other bishops who are summoned to the meetings in turn.

148. Patriarch Alexis II, head of the Russian Orthodox Church since 1990, leaves the Annunciation Cathedral in the Moscow Kremlin.

149. Repairing the Diveev Monastery in the Nizhny Novgorod (Gorky) region. Over the past two decades, efforts have been made to reopen and restore the thousands of churches which fell into disrepair during the anti-religious period.

150. A monk looks down on on the Nilova Pustyn Monastery on Lake Selinger, north-west of Moscow. Many urban monasteries were founded between 1200 and 1350, after which the emphasis was on the building of monasteries in remote areas, many of which had a colonizing and semi-military function.

151. Reverence for the icon is an essential element of Russian Orthodox ritual, dating back to the tenth century, when icons were brought from Byzantium to Russia. The most intense devotion is offered to images of Christ and the Holy Mother of God, but those of the saints and feasts of the Church are also revered.

152. Lighting a votive candle. Candles have great symbolic significance in Orthodox worship: a single one represents the saint in front of whose icon it stands; three together represent the Trinity; seven, the gifts of the Holy Ghost. Money from the sale of candles goes towards the upkeep of the church.

153. The face of faith: a monk in the cathedral of Donskoy Monastery. The Russian clergy are divided into 'white' and 'black'. The former live in the community and can marry and have children, while the latter are celibate monks, from whose ranks are chosen the higher clergy: bishops, archbishops and metropolitans.

154. On the eve of Easter, the faithful have brought offerings to be blessed at the Donskoy Monastery in Moscow: Easter cake (kulich), Easter cheese (paskha) and painted eggs. For the Orthodox Church, Easter is the most important feast. The service begins two hours before midnight and ends with Mass in the early hours of Easter Sunday.

155. *The power of prayer. Nuns of the*
Kozalsk Convent close to Kaluga, south of
Moscow, pray daily for the whole world.

*156. Nuns singing in a choir. The use of
instruments is forbidden in the Russian
Church, which has an ancient polyphonic
choral tradition.*

157. Of the 1,105 monasteries and convents existing in 1917, only six monasteries and 10 convents remained in 1986, kept alive by the faith of nuns like these at the Zolotonosha Convent.

158. A village woman kisses the hand of her parish priest, who belongs to the 'white clergy'. Under Communism, his role was strictly confined to spiritual matters and he was not allowed to exert any wider influence in the community.

159, 160. Nuns at the Zolotonska Convent bringing in the milk and tending a calf. Manual labour is accepted as a natural part of convent life. Since most nuns are from rural families, they are accustomed to farmwork.

161. Bells are rung to announce the beginning and end of every church service. Russians were famous for their skill in casting bells, whose chimes are echoed in the work of many celebrated Russian composers of the nineteenth century.

162. Besides devotion to a life of prayer, obedience, poverty and chastity, nuns and monks are expected to perform all manner of daily tasks, for monastic communities must be self-supporting as far as possible.

For the first time since 1917, free elections were held: on 26 March 1989 the first multi-candidate elections resulted in defeats for scores of Communists. A subsequent electoral achievement for anti-conservatism was the landslide victory of Gorbachev's rival, Boris Yeltsin, in Moscow in 1990. The state also undertook to draft a new constitution and a new Union treaty.

In the meantime the Soviet Union had suffered two major catastrophes. The Chernobyl nuclear reactor disaster in April 1986, about which the authorities failed to issue proper warning, left huge areas of the Ukraine and Belorussia with hazardous levels of high radiation affecting over a million people. In December 1988, a devastating earthquake struck in Armenia, killing some 80,000 people and leaving tens of thousands homeless. Gorbachev's attempts to revive the ramshackle economy, plagued by obsolescent machinery, low productivity, overmanning and general inefficiency, had met with widespread resistance: there had been strikes in the mining districts and elsewhere.

The Soviet Union was showing signs of falling apart. To gain the support and economic assistance from the West essential to carry out his reforms, Gorbachev had to renounce the Brezhnev Doctrine, withdraw Soviet forces from Afghanistan, and loosen the Kremlin's hold on the East European states and non-Russian republics of the Soviet Union. Beginning with Hungary, one by one the countries of the eastern bloc broke free and opened their borders with the West, where, in contrast to his reputation at home, Gorbachev's popularity was increasing (on 15 October 1990 he was named as recipient of the Nobel Peace Prize). The fall of the Berlin Wall in winter 1989 had been the symbolic first step leading to the reunification of Germany and the relaxation of East-West tension. Inside the Soviet Union, republics such as Estonia, Lithuania and Latvia demanded independence. Their hopes were raised by the Party congress in June 1988, which ended with a resolution regarding the rights of the Union republics. Afterwards, however, the Kremlin backtracked. A new decree giving the Supreme Soviet the power to overrule the republics caused outrage in the Baltic states, which defiantly declared their independence from the central power of Moscow. Henceforth, successive new drafts of the Union Treaty were rejected by the governments of the Baltic states, Moldavia, Armenia and Georgia.

Finally, three years later, a more acceptable version was scheduled to be signed on 19 August 1991. But the day before, a group of high-ranking Communist hardliners, angry at the Soviet Union's loss of influence and the erosion the centralized power structure, had organised a coup. The junta formed an Emergency Committee, broadcasting an announcement that President Gorbachev (under house arrest in the Crimea) was seriously ill and a state of emergency had been declared.

The Emergency Committee's plans to arrest Boris Yeltsin, the recently elected president of the Russian Republic, miscarried, since he had been forewarned of their intentions. He promptly made his way to the Parliament building (the 'White House') in Moscow, from where he led opposition to the coup. Meanwhile, the people of the city of Moscow and the Russian Federation, suddenly reminded of their vulnerability to arbitrary and repressive actions, mounted a tense show of moral and military resistance. In Moscow barricades were built, cobblestones were dug up, and tanks of uncertain loyalty roamed streets. A crowd several thousand strong milled around the Parliament building in pouring rain to defend Yeltsin and their freedom. When military leaders refused to order their troops to fire on civilians, the coup collapsed, and its leaders were themselves arrested.

163. The Old Testament Trinity, otherwise known as The Hospitality of Abraham, by Andrei Rublev, c. 1410. The most famous of Russian icon painters, the monk Rublev, who lived for twenty years in the Donskoy Monastery in Moscow, was responsible for the decoration with icons and frescoes of several cathedrals, among them the Annunciation Cathedral in the Moscow Kremlin and the Dormition Cathedral in Vladimir.

The End of the Soviet State

The remaining months of the Soviet Union's existence were marked by the rise in popularity of Boris Yeltsin, the hero of the resistance in Moscow, and the efforts of Mikhail Gorbachev to preserve the Union. Outmanoeuvred by Yeltsin, who took the lead in abolishing the Communist Party, he was powerless to influence events. On 8 December 1990, the three leaders of the former Union Republics, Boris Yeltsin of Russia, Leonid Kravchuk of Ukraine and Stanislav Shushkevich of Belorussia (Belarus), signed the Bialowieza Treaty, which officially proclaimed the end of the Soviet Union and the creation of the Commonwealth of Independent States. This was followed by a meeting in Alma Ata on 21 December, when the three were joined by the leaders of eight other republics of the former U.S.S.R. (Armenia, Azerbaijan, Kirgistan, Kazakstan, Moldova, Turkmenistan, Tajikistan and Uzbekistan), who signed an agreement to join the CIS as 'co-founders'. Lithuania, Latvia, Estonia and Georgia had already chosen not to join. Four days later, President Gorbachev resigned and the next day the Supreme Soviet formally dissolved itself. The Red Flag was lowered from the Kremlin buildings and the Russian tricolour hoisted in its place.

The months and years ahead would be very difficult. With the disintegration of the Soviet Union and abolition of the Communist Party, the Russian Federation was suddenly left without the structures that had kept it intact for seventy years. The workings of virtually all the state and economic institutions had to be reconsidered. Should anarchy again triumph, to judge from history it would not be long before a new despotism arrived. Perhaps the last word should be given to the Russian Cosmonaut, Sergei Krikalev, who was marooned in space for three hundred and ten days while economic, territorial and bureaucratic battles raged beneath him. While he was circling the earth, his homeland had changed its name, its flag, and its anthem. When he landed on 26 March 1992, it was to a country very different from the one he had left ten months earlier.

The mail-boat SS Peter I crossing the Black Sea, nineteenth-century engraving.

THE ARTS

Literature

Russia has suffered terribly this century, but, perhaps because of this, her poets have been remarkable. The tragedy is that so few of them survived to carry on Russia's great literary tradition. To quote from the autobiography of the great opera singer Galina Vishnevskaya: 'What a horrible fate the poets of Soviet Russia have had: Gumiliev was shot; Blok starved to death; Esenin committed suicide; Mayakovsky shot himself; Mandelstam died in a labour camp; Tsvetaeva hanged herself; Pasternak was driven into the grave; Akhmatova was hounded and didn't publish for many years.' Just as the Germans are considered a musical nation, and the French and Italians are celebrated for the fine arts, the Russians are famed for their literature: the weight of the written word is tremendous in a country with few other certainties.

The Russian language, belonging to the East Slavic group, is close to Polish, Ukrainian and Belorussian. Sonorous and expressive, its roots are in Byzantine-influenced Church Slavonic (still used for the Russian Orthodox Church liturgy), but it absorbed many Tatar words while Russia was under Tatar rule. Its vocabulary was greatly expanded during the reign of Peter the Great, when the alphabet was simplified and over three thousand new foreign words came into parlance. More recently, American-English has been a major source of loan-words.

Many years have come and gone since the literary tastes of old Muscovy were discarded in favour of those of Western Europe, ushering in the 'Golden Age' of Russian literature. The eighteenth-century classical poet, Sumarokov, had shyly learned his role and bequeathed the lyre to Alexander Pushkin (1799-1837), the father of Russian letters, whose prophetic appearance, in the words of Dostoevsky, one of his most eminent successors, 'helped to illuminate our obscure path with a new guiding light.'

Pushkin, Russia's most famous poet was the author of over seven hundred lyric poems, as well as volumes of narrative poetry, dramatic works, short stories, a correspondence of over eight hundred letters, and adaptations of Russian fairy tales that every Russian reads as a child. It is one of Russia's tragedies that Pushkin, goaded by court gossip into a fatal duel over his wife's honour, died when he was only thirty-seven years old, in the full bloom of his creative power. A young hussar officer, Mikhail Lermontov, reacting to the destruction of his country's greatest poet, wrote an elegy, expressing his wrath against society and his sorrow at the 'prophet's lips now sealed'. Enthusiastically received by the public, the verses of 'The Death of a Poet' displeased the authorities. Lermontov was arrested for his apparent call for revolution, court-martialled, and exiled to the Caucasus. Within four years, the rebellious poet was also killed in a duel, on 15 July 1841.

Lermontov, in fact, never met Pushkin, though he had long been an ardent admirer of his poetry. Above all, Lermontov wrote of the Caucasus. He loved the solemn glory of wild nature and the flood of sunset between the icy peaks. It was there that he set his most celebrated work, *A Hero of Our Time*, a novel consisting of five short stories, each self-contained, but each revealing an aspect of the character of the hero, Pechorin, a rich, worldly, and possibly disgraced young officer. So remarkable is Lermontov's use of language and his impeccable craftsmanship that Anton Chekhov recommended anyone to read the first chapter of the novel in order to learn how to write.

Russian literature is noted for its satire. Besides Ivan Krylov (1769-1844), Russia's answer to La Fontaine, another master of the art of ridicule was Ukrainian-born Nicholas Gogol (1809-1852). When Gogol arrived in

Alexander Pushkin (1799-1837).

St Petersburg as a young man, Pushkin encouraged him in his career as a writer, whose gifts (in Gogol's own words) lay in portraying 'the self-satisfaction of vulgar people'. Best known as the author of *The Government Inspector* and *Dead Souls*, Gogol is renowned for telling a few bitter home truths about Russia's troubles. After reading *Dead Souls*, Pushkin famously exclaimed: 'Lord, how sad is our Russia!' There is almost no better-known ending in Russian literature than the conclusion of the first volume of *Dead Souls*: an enigmatic image of Russia as a flying troika, speeding no-one knows where.

Some characters in books outshine their creators. One such figure from nineteenth-century Russian literature is Ilya Oblomov, the archetypal lethargic and dreamy aristocrat created by Ivan Goncharov (1812-91), one of the new generation of writers of Russia's Golden Age. Life drifts tranquilly past Oblomov until he falls in love with a girl called Olga and she with him. But their marriage never takes place, for Oblomov is incapable of summoning up the energy to make the necessary arrangements. Olga, tired of waiting, marries someone else, and Oblomov relapses into his dressing-gown and slippers, cared for his devoted housekeeper, whom he eventually marries.

Europe discovered Russian literature through the novels of Ivan Turgenev (1818-83), which were translated into several languages long before the works of any other Russian writer. His masterpiece, *Fathers and Sons,* is, in the words of the English critic, Maurice Baring, 'as beautifully constructed as a drama of Sophocles'. Equally lyrical, and at the same time evocative of adult passion, is the novella *First Love* (1860). Turgenev, who has been called the Schumann of Russian literature, first found readers with his *Sportsman's Sketches,* and became famous with his *Nest of Gentlefolk* (1859).

Fedor Dostoevsky (1821-81) established his name as a writer with his novel, *Crime and Punishment*, published in 1866, which made him famous not only at home but far beyond the borders of Russia. Dostoevsky's method of taking us from the 'real to the more real' (to quote from the Russian thinker, Viacheslav Ivanov) is displayed in this 'psychological study of a crime'. The hero, Raskolnikov, is an example of a Nihilist who despises conventional morals. An impoverished former student of St Petersburg University, overburdened by theories, he decides to kill an old woman money-lender: she is stupid and wicked, and would anyway probably not live for more than a few months. But no sooner has the crime been committed than Raskolnikov experiences hitherto undreamt-of feelings of repentance, eventually giving himself up against his own will. In this compelling work, Dostoevsky gave the world a perception of the anarchic Russian character, deeply divided against himself. It was a type that fascinated the author. As he wrote in his *Diary of a Writer*: 'The Russian always feels impelled to overstep the bounds, to go to the very edge of the precipice and lean over and scan its depths; often enough to hurl himself over it like a madman. It is that hungering after negation which besets the man of greatest faith...'

Dostoevsky is often compared with Count Lev Tolstoy (1828-1910), another of Russia's greatest thinkers and one of the world's supreme novelists. The secret of Tolstoy's literary technique lay in his truthfulness to life. 'A Tolstoyan tree,' wrote the critic, George Steiner, 'shadows the ground more solidly, with greater feel of dappled light, of leaf-mould, than does any other tree in literature, and very nearly, in common sensation.'

Tolstoy's own life, ending with his dramatic flight from home, is a story in itself. He was born in 1828 at the family estate of Yasnaya Polyana,

125 miles from Moscow. As a young man, he served in the army in the Caucasus and the Crimea, and it was then that he wrote his first stories and impressions. Following his marriage to Sophia Behrs in 1862, he spent the next fifteen years in the countryside, finishing *War and Peace* in 1869 and *Anna Karenina* in 1877. Two years later, the thoughts that had long been tormenting Tolstoy came to the fore in a spiritual crisis, described in *A Confession*. There followed the massive prophetic tracts, giving his views on religion and on non-resistance to evil. Rejecting what he regarded as the foolish, nasty inventions of urban civilization, Tolstoy advocated a return to the simplicity of primitive agricultural life. Increasingly unhappy about the fact that he was living in conditions of great luxury while surrounded by poverty, Tolstoy eventually left Yasnaya Polyana forever at the age of eighty-two.

Among Tolstoy's contemporaries, four of the finest prose writers were the philosopher Vassily Rozanov (1856-1919), Anton Chekhov (1860-1904), Ivan Bunin (1870-1935) and Maxim Gorky (1868-1936). Anton Chekhov, praised by Tolstoy as 'an incomparable artist' has perhaps acquired the greatest fame world-wide. Like Somerset Maugham, another master of the short story, Chekhov trained as a doctor, but the success of his literary works won him over to letters. 'Medicine is my legal spouse, while literature is my mistress,' he wrote in 1866. By 1888 Chekhov had become a thoroughly committed professional writer, yet he did not abandon medicine entirely, serving as a doctor at his country estate, Melikhovo, near Moscow and undertaking a trip to the penal colony of Sakhalin in 1890. When his own health began to fail, he moved to the Crimea, and after 1900 most of his life was spent at Yalta, where his house has now been turned into a museum. His best-known short stories and plays were written in the last years of his life, when he met and married Olga Knipper, an actress at the Moscow Arts Theatre. But their happy marriage was brief: Chekhov died of tuberculosis shortly afterwards in 1904.

Around the turn of the century, a brilliant new generation of prose writers and poets was emerging, whose achievements contributed to the 'Silver Age' of Russian culture in the years between 1885 and 1915. But Russia was hurtling towards revolution and, swept up in events, many of the gifted new writers either fled into exile, were stifled by the new bureaucracy or were driven to their deaths before they had time to hand on the torch to future generations, with disastrous consequences for Russian culture. As Osip Mandelstam wrote: 'If only two or three generations are dumb, it could lead Russia to historical death.'

Osip Mandelstam was born in 1891 and died in a transit camp near Vladivostok probably at the end of 1938. His gifts as a poet were immediately recognised with the publication of his first book of poetry in 1913. Later he would write five major prose works. Throughout most of his life he owned nothing but a few books and some clothing; he composed his poems in his mind while walking. In the hell-house that Russia became under Stalin, the poet was arrested and died a 'non-person' at the age of forty-seven.

One of Mandelstam's closest friends was the *grande dame* of Russian letters, Anna Akhmatova, who was also a victim of her times. Her first husband, the poet Gumiliev, was shot, and her son and second husband were both imprisoned during the Thirties. Her early poems, remarkable for their simplicity and grandeur, were love lyrics, but she is better known for her later works: *Requiem*, *From Six Books* and *Poem without a Hero*, a response to the sufferings of the purges and her own personal tragedy.

A contemporary of Akhmatova was Boris Pasternak, born in

Moscow in 1890 into a talented family: his father, a friend of Tolstoy, was a leading Russian painter, his mother an outstanding pianist. They moved in a cultured circle and were in close touch with European trends. In his masterpiece, *Doctor Zhivago*, he would describe through the life of his hero how the Revolution swept away this order and the new 'homeless' age was born. Like everyone else, Pasternak found it hard to survive: by the Thirties, writing had become such a dangerous profession that he turned to translating poetry as a safer livelihood. When *Doctor Zhivago* was rejected for publication in the Soviet Union in the Fifties, he agreed to allow the novel to appear abroad in an Italian translation in 1957. Pasternak's nomination for the Nobel Prize for literature the following year provoked a fierce Soviet campaign against him and he was threatened with forfeiture of his citizenship. Having declined the prize, he was allowed to stay in Russia, but died a year and a half later.

Two others who rank among the outstanding Russian writers of the twentieth century are the popular humorist Mikhail Zoshchenko (1895-1958) and, of course, Mikhail Bulgakov (1891-1940), best known abroad as the author of *The Master and Margarita*.

In 1934, the Communist Party had founded the Union of Writers. Those writers who conformed to the system were accepted as members and became part of a privileged elite; those who did not were excluded from both union membership and any chance of being published. The Union offered patronage and financial support, but in return demanded subservience to the Party line and socialist realism. The latter was described by the satirist Vladimir Voinovich (expelled from the Union in 1974) as 'praise of the leaders in terms they can understand'.

The lack of a free press and publishing led to the phenomenon of *samizdat*: manuscripts of books, copies of typescripts, petitions or poetry were circulated at first among close friends and then to a wider public. Among the most significant works of fiction to appear first in *samizdat* were Solzhenitsyn's *First Circle* and *Cancer Ward*, *The Life and Extraordinary Adventures of Private Ivan Chonkin* by Voinovich, and Nadezhda Mandelstam's *Hope against Hope* and *Hope Abandoned*. Against this background, Russia produced some outstanding literary figures still little known in the West, such as the writer and critic Andrei Platanov (1899-1951) and the poet Nikolai Zabolotsky (1903-58).

There have been five Russian Nobel prize winners for literature: Ivan Bunin, Boris Pasternak, Mikhail Sholokhov, Alexander Solzhenitsyn and Josif Brodsky.

Architecture

There is no more typical and delightful Russian scene than the glittering onion-domes of churches set in a landscape blanketed in snow. With its central dome surrounded by cupolas, like a broody mother-hen nestling over her little chicks, a Russian church represents a comforting rallying point in the otherwise intimidating, unprotected plain.

Russia borrowed its early architecture, like its icon painting, from Byzantium. From the eleventh to the thirteenth centuries, early towns tended to be built on defensible sites on high river banks, commanding the surroundings and visible from afar. Low, white walls, with bold and regularly spaced towers, enclosed churches with brilliant domes, and bell towers. The finest examples of traditional architecture can be seen in the towns of Yaroslavl, Kostroma, Vladimir, Suzdal, Bogolyubovo and Zagorsk.

Siberian Crown (above) and Monomakh Crown.

In such a heavily forested country, the most natural building material has always been timber. Traditionally, Russian carpenters embellished the diverse structures they were building, from log-cabins, barns and windmills to large houses, fortress towers, huge cathedrals, churches and monasteries, with elaborately carved decorations above windows and porches. The most majestic surviving examples of wooden church architecture are to be found on the island of Kizhi in Lake Onega: the grand and gracefully silhouetted multi-domed Cathedral of the Transfiguration and the ten-domed Church of the Intercession with its bell tower and a palisade with elaborate turreted gates. Wooden architecture predominates in northern Russia and in some of the older settlements and towns of Siberia, such as Tyumen,where wood-carvers won renown as early as the seventeenth century.

One of the jewels of Russian architecture is the Moscow Kremlin (fortress), with its cathedrals, its many towers and its crenelated, red-brick walls, the last raised by an Italian architect in the fifteenth century. The oldest part of the Kremlin is Cathedral Square and its three grand cathedrals: the white-stone colossus of the Cathedral of the Assumption (*Uspensky sobor*, 1475-79) on the north side, protecting the little Church of the Deposition of the Robe (1484-86) beside it; the Annunciation Cathedral (*Blagoveshchensky sobor*, 1484-89) by master-builders from Pskov on the south side; and the Cathedral of the Archangel Michael (*Arkhangelsky sobor*, 1505-08) on the south-eastern corner.

The Kremlin walls enclose several palaces. The Patriarch's Palace, immediately north of the Assumption Cathedral, built in the mid-seventeenth century for Patriarch Nikon, is a now museum of Russian seventeenth-century life. On the west side of Cathedral Square, standing next to the seventeenth-century Terem Palace with its golden domes and chequered roof, is the Faceted Palace, designed by two Italian architects as a setting for the imperial throne room and for sumptuous banquets. Other notable buildings in the Kremlin include the Armoury Museum, containing a magnificent collection of treasures, and the marble, glass and concrete Palace of Congresses, the only modern structure, built in the early Sixties for Communist Party congresses.

Just outside the Kremlin walls, on the edge of windswept Red Square, stands the Church of the Intercession of the Virgin (*Sobor Pokrova*), better known as St Basil's, one of the world's most astonishing and bizarre buildings. It was built by two Russian architects between 1555 and 1560 for Ivan the Terrible, to commemorate his victory over the Tatar khanate of Kazan.

The reign of the dynamic Peter the Great provided an encouraging atmosphere for the construction of both secular and religious buildings. Churches and monasteries changed in appearance with the adoption of the western, Baroque style. Great parks and gardens were laid out in new ways and on a large scale. In 1703, the foundations were laid of a new capital, St Petersburg, envisaged by its creator, Peter the Great, as a purely western city. Raised with astonishing speed along the banks of the Neva and its tributaries, the town was intersected by wide canals, and the streets were regularly planned, in contrast to the sprawling forms of older cities. The Peter Paul Fortress, founded in May 1703, is the oldest building in the city. Its massive walls enclose the Cathedral of SS Peter and Paul, built by the Italian architect, Trezzini, between 1714 and 1725, with its golden spire, crowned by an unusual weather-vane in the form of an angel holding a cross.

Its counterpart is the golden spire topped by an aerial ship above the Admiralty building, far away on the other side of the Neva. The Admiralty, a large shipyard that also played a defensive role, was the second major building project in St Petersburg. Originally a wooden structure, in the 1720s it was rebuilt in stone by the architect, Ivan Korobov, who emphasized the main entrance by adding a three-tiered tower. The present neo-classical Admiralty building, dating from 1806-15, which retained Korobov's original layout, was designed by Adreyan Zakharov.

The celebrated Italian architect, Bartolemeo Rastrelli, working in the Baroque style, left his mark on St Petersburg in the middle of the eighteenth century. His buildings include the grand imperial residence at Tsarskoye Selo, the Winter Palace and the Smolny Convent, as well as many palaces on a smaller scale for the nobility. The Winter Palace, commissioned by the Empress Elizabeth and built between 1754 and 1762, is perhaps his most remarkable achievement, a stunning example of Russian Baroque.

In the reign of Catherine II, whose taste in architecture was for a more sober style, the Winter Palace was altered and extended. The Frenchman, Vallin de la Mothe, designed for her the Small Hermitage, connected to the palace by a passageway, as her private retreat. Next to this, Yury Velten, a German by origin, then built the Old Hermitage, facing the Neva, and Giacomo Quarenghi, another Italian architect, added the Hermitage Theatre in neo-classical style to the eastern side of the palace between 1782 and 1785. The extensions to the eastern side were to house the Empress's growing collection of European art. The Winter Palace remained an imperial residence until 1917, after which the whole complex was turned into a museum: the State Hermitage, one of the largest art galleries in the world.

By the end of the eighteenth century, St Petersburg was a majestic and still expanding city, now dominated by the neo-classical style, which had taken over from the Baroque. This found expression in the work of many architects, both Russian and foreign. Prominent among them were Ivan Starov, who was responsible for Holy Trinity Cathedral in the Alexander Nevsky Monastery, and the Italian, Carlo Rossi, who designed several grand sweeps of classical buildings around the city. The designs for Nevsky Prospect, the city's main thoroughfare, running two and a half miles from the Admiralty to the Alexander Nevsky Monastery, were drawn up as early as 1713, the year in which the monastery was founded, and were modelled on some famous avenues in Paris and Versailles. One by one, many fine buildings were erected on Nevsky Prospect. Outstanding among them is the great, colonnaded Kazan Cathedral, built at the very beginning of the nineteenth century by the architect Andrei Voronikhin, who intended it to be as majestic as St Peter's in Rome. St Petersburg set an example for Russian architecture to follow. From the late eighteenth century onwards, the classical style predominated, and building work proceeded on an enormous scale.

After the middle of the nineteenth century, patronage of the arts moved to Moscow, the home of the new merchant princes. While Pavel Tretyakov was assembling his magnificent collection of Russian paintings, his brother-in-law, the industrialist Savva Mamontov, created a rural retreat for artists, architects and designers at his country home of Abramtsevo, just north of Moscow. This project was influential in developing the Arts and Crafts movement and the revival of a national architectural style with traditional forms and ornamentation. Architecture took a markedly new direction at the turn of the century in the work of the Fedor Shekhtel, a friend of Anton Chekhov and a successful theatre designer before he devoted his energies to architecture in the Style Moderne or Art Nouveau, as it is more often called in the West. Besides his unique building of the Yaroslavl Railway Station in Moscow, probably Shekhtel's masterpiece was the two-

166. Dogs are widely used for pulling sleds in the north of Russia. Among Siberian tribes such as the Koryaks, they were sacrificed regularly to appease the spirits. The Koryaks also believed that dogs guarded the entrance to the other world, so that a man who during his lifetime had ill-treated his dogs would be refused entrance.

167. A herder collects reindeer for sleds at Palana, north-east Kamchatka. One or two reindeer are taken from every herd, tamed and used for riding or drawing sleds.

168. *Ice-fishing on the Bering Sea, near Tilchiki. The indigenous peoples of Kamchatka, the Itelmen, Chukchi and Koryaks, are accustomed and adapted to the nine long months of winter in their native region.*

169. *Praying for a catch! In the remote north-eastern regions of Russia, people survive on a staple winter diet of boiled reindeer meat and dried fish, supplemented by tea, sugar, salt, noodles and potatoes flown in by helicopter.*

170. Longboat on the Bikin River, south of Khabarovsk in the Primorsky Kray (Coastal Region), close to the border with Manchuria.

171. The tundra, a Finnish word meaning 'barren crests of mountains', is patterned by thousands of lakes and rivers.

172. The snow-clad Koryakskaya volcano (11,432 ft, overleaf). Geologically speaking, Kamchatka is young. More than half the peninsula is covered witht the results of volcanic eruptions.

173. Mist over the chain of volcanoes close to Petropavlovsk-Kamchatsky. This range has several active craters that expel fountains of red hot lava, cinder clouds and jets of steam and gas.

174. *A deadly acid lake fills the crater of the extinct Karilsky volcano. Its waters, like those of other crater lakes, contain sulphuric and hydrochloric acids, and are coloured turquoise blue by the suspended particles of sulphur.*

175. Tundra landscape at Tigil Kovran, north-west Kamchatka, close to the Sea of Okhotsk, which separates the peninsula from the Khabarovsk region on the Asian mainland.

176. The solitude of the tundra. Patterned by thousands of lakes and rivers, this is the northernmost zone of Russia, sweeping across 3,000 mi., all the way from Finland to the Pacific Ocean.

177. How many secrets the taiga conceals within its depths! But in the foreseeable future, forests like this one near the Bikin River in the Primorsky Kray (Coastal Region) of the southern Far East, will disappear unless selective felling and reforestation schemes are introduced.

178. The taiga is Russia's equivalent to the rainforest in terms of timber resources. Composed mainly of spruce and pine, it grows over a small part of north European Russia and most of Siberia and the Far East; in all, an area of about eight million square miles.

179. Hunting walrus and seal is an age-old activity of the maritime tribes, like the Chukchi, living in north-eastern Siberia. Traditionally, the 'boatful' was made up of eight oarsmen and one helmsman, known as the 'boatmaster'. The meat from the catch would be divided equally among all on board, while the head and tusks of walrus would go to the master, reappearing in due course for ceremonial rituals.

180,181. Siberian tribes venerated the walrus, sometimes described as the 'Lord of the Sea'. When they feared being attacked, they used special incantations to induce the creatures to spare the boat. The maritime Chukchi often made sacrifices to a sea-spirit called the Mother of the Walrus, armed with two tusks, who lived on the bottom of the sea.

182. *A Koryak girl beating a deerskin drum. Dancing and singing, imitating the movements of waves and grass and the sounds of birds and animals, are part of the traditions of the Koryaks in northern Kamchatka.*

183. *A Koryak from Palana, Kamchatka. After sixty years of collectivization, the reindeer herders are returning to their old homes abandoned because of a government decision to concentrate natives in central townships and assign them to state farms.*

184. Two friends from the village of Kovran, north-west Kamchatka. The girl on the left is Russian, the other is one of the last pure Itelmen, of whom there are only 1,500 left in Kovran.

186. A Koryak dog-sled driver. Along with reindeer racing, dog-sled racing is an increasingly popular sport in Kamchatka.

185. Chukchi herders, Khailino, Kamchatka. Despite their cheerful grins, they face great hardships: food supplies to their camps are irregular and health care for themselves and their herds is poor.

187. Reindeer seek fresh grazing in the tundra during the summer months (overleaf). The animal is all important in the culture of the native peoples of the north-east. The Chukchi have 20 different terms to describe the reindeer, depending on their sex, the shape of their horns and their body size.

188. Summer reindeer camp at Kluchi, in
the Koryak Okrug of Kamchatka. Reindeer
primarily graze on lichens, especially
species of Cladonia, better known as 'reindeer moss'. Herds are constantly on the
move as grazing is quickly exhausted. The
moss grows so slowly it takes ten years for
the vegetation to regenerate.

189. A reindeer herder. In spring and early
summer, he will drive his animals for hundreds of miles along traditional routes to
the Arctic Ocean coast. On the way, the
females will give birth to their calves.

190. *A fisherman/herder from the village of Kailino, Kamchatka (left).*

191. *Above, three generations of a native Kamchatkan family.*

193. Air drying of salmon at Khalilino, Kamchatka. In the past, local fishermen who did not store enough dried fish (yuko-la) in summer, starved during the winter. Now, the fishermen dry salmon to sell on to the herders.

192, 194. Beside the River Vyvenko, salmon roe, from which red caviar is made, is extracted by skilled fingers. Kamchatka's rivers abound in salmon: the total catch is nearly 1.5 million tons a year. The first salmon-processing factory was built at the mouth of the Kamchatka River in 1896.

195. *Not the Mississippi but boats on the Amur River at Khabarovsk, Russia's premier far eastern city. From here the great Amur flows westward, demarcating much of the Sino-Russian border.*

196. Fishing trawler on remote Ossora Bay, north-east Kamchatka. These ships are floating factories, in whose holds the catch is prepared for sale on the international market.

197. Young seal on an ice-floe. The Commander Islands off Kamchatka are among the world's major seal-breeding areas. There are some 300,000 in the breeding grounds on the islands, which are protected from uncontrolled hunting.

storey mansion he designed for the industrialist Ryabushinsky in 1900, which later belonged to the writer Maxim Gorky, and is now a museum.

By the second decade of the twentieth century, the Style Moderne had fallen out of favour and Russian architects began reverting to the tradition of classicism. For a brief period after the Revolution, the flourishing of the Avant-Garde in the arts was reflected in buildings with original, bold, geometric designs using new materials. But as the political climate became increasingly repressive under Stalin, a heavy, monumental type of neo-classicism predominated in the 1930s and 1940s, followed in the Fifties by Stalin's grandiose, wedding-cake skyscrapers reminiscent from a distance of Gothic cathedrals. In the post-Stalin era, the International Modern style gradually appeared in the cities.

Fine Arts

Russian art is little known and appreciated abroad, apart from the glorious school of icon painting that emerged in the fifteenth century and the Avant-Garde movement that sprang up between 1906 and 1924, becoming one of the most vital currents in modern western art, at the forefront of the development of abstraction. In between and since then, many painters and sculptors contributed to the creation of a national school of Russian art: the portraitists of the eighteenth century were followed by the genre and realist painters of the nineteenth. After 1934 the dominant style was Socialist Realism, but an underground art movement developed in the Sixties, and since the late Seventies contemporary Russian art is much better known abroad.

From the eleventh to the beginning of the eighteenth century, artistic creativity reflected the atmosphere of awe and mystery that enveloped the Orthodox Church. The most important form of early Russian art was the icon, though there was also a large amount of fresco painting, much of which has been lost. The word *ikon* means 'image' in Greek, but in the Christian era the term came to be used exclusively for religious pictures of Christ or saints on a wooden panel. Having passed from the Greek to the Slav world with the spread of Christianity, icons were produced in large numbers and used to decorate churches, mostly placed on the iconostasis, the wall or screen separating the congregation from the sanctuary. From the mid-fourteenth century it was in Russia that the finest icons were produced, and it is around that time that a specific national style can be distinguished. Russian icon painting reached the pinnacle of its achievement in the mid-fifteenth century in the work of Theophanes the Greek, Andrei Rublev and Dionisy. A later master, working in the seventeenth century, was Simon Ushakov, but after him most icons were copies of earlier works. Often they were embellished with metal halos, or metal casings, decorated with precious stones and metals.

From the eighteenth century onwards, when Peter the Great introduced western tastes and forms in art and architecture, Russian art moved away from religion towards a secular tradition, with painters emulating western styles and studying abroad. Portrait painting, marine and townscapes were the dominant *genres*, but in the second half of the nineteenth century artists of the Wanderers group started painting scenes of contemporary life. It was not long before Russian painters began concentrating on neglected aspects of their heritage, such as folk art, a trend similar to that of the Arts and Crafts movements in Europe, and there was a vogue for religious and historical subjects.

198. *'Altogether elsewhere, vast*
Herds of reindeer move across
Miles and miles of golden moss,
Silently and very fast.'
W.H.Auden: 'The Fall of Rome'

The beginning of the twentieth century was a period of great experimentation in art, as in literature and architecture. One new artistic movement swept away another, from Neo-primitivism and Cubo-futurism to Suprematism and Constructivism. The icon, that most traditional form of Russian art, somewhat surprisingly exerted an influence on Russian Avant-Garde, for not only were some artists familiar with techniques of icon painting, having worked in icon studios, but in 1913 a remarkable exhibition of icons was held in Moscow, which led to a revival of interest in this art form. Remembering how icons call people to God not through mirroring real life, but through the resonance of their colours and through an assemblage of different textures, the Avant-Garde experimented with the expressive qualities of the materials themselves in order to create images of beauty. Among the first to develop abstract art were Vladimir Tatlin (1885-1953), Kazimir Malevich (1878-1935) and Vassily Kandinsky (1866-1921).

The activity of the Avant-Garde went into decline in the early Thirties under the pressure of Socialist Realism. After 1934 artists were supposed to abandon 'formalism' and produce works demonstrating the happiness, optimism and achievements of Soviet society. A favoured artist from this period was Alexander Samokhvalov, whose paintings depicting the building of new Metro stations and factories were reproduced and distributed throughout the Soviet Union in the late Thirties and Forties. Sculptors were commissioned to produce numerous monumental works glorifying workers, the armed forces, war heroes, and of course, the Soviet leaders, above all, Lenin and Stalin.

Music

Until the nineteenth century, musical expression found its outlet primarily in the choral music of the Russian Orthodox Church and in the varied and beautiful folk music. The Orthodox Church has always forbidden the use of musical instruments in worship and for this reason a polyphonic musical style developed in medieval times. The techniques of European harmony and the essentials of the theory behind it were assimilated through Polish-trained singers who took their knowledge with them to Moscow and St Petersburg in the seventeenth century. The tradition of choral singing accounts, in part, for the popularity of opera in Russia and the importance of the chorus in Russian operatic works.

Nothing is more powerfully evocative of the land and its people, more typically Russian, than the the strains of a balalaika. Early Russian folk music, played on a range of bowed, plucked and wind instruments, including the sixteenth-century *domra*, a forerunner of the balalaika, and the *gusli*, a primitive fiddle on which minstrels used to accompany their songs, was an inspiration to the great Russian composers of the nineteenth century. This common source accounts for the recognizably national character of much of their work.

It was Mikhail Glinka (1804-57) who laid the foundation for modern Russian music. After three years of study in Italy, he apparently began to suffer from what he called 'musical homesickness' — the wish to hear music expressing the temperament of his own people. His two best-known operas, *Ivan Susanin* and *Ruslan and Ludmila*, were based on Russian folklore and historical legend. Glinka's works inspired a group of five younger composers who emerged as an extraordinary musical phenomenon in the late nineteenth century: Mily Balakirev (1836-1910); Alexander Borodin (1833-87); Cesar Cui (1833-1918); Modest Mussorgsky (1839-81); and

Don Cossack woman, nineteenth century.

Nikolai Rimsky-Korsakov (1844-1908). All of them composed in snatches, obliged by circumstances to earn a living at some more lucrative profession. Balakirev began his career as a mathematician; Cui was an army officer; Rimsky-Korsakov was in the navy; Mussorgsky started in the army and then became a minor civil servant; Borodin was a chemist, and also became a champion of women's education. Perhaps because their attention was so often distracted, the 'Mighty Five' composers left unfinished a remarkable number of important works. Borodin's opera *Prince Igor*, for example, was completed by Rimsky-Korsakov and Glazunov, while Mussorgsky's famous opera *Boris Godunov* was revised by Rimsky-Korsakov and, at a later date, by Shostakovich.

Peter Ilyich Tchaikovsky (1840-93), the best-known of all Russian composers, gave up a position in the civil service at twenty-three to devote himself entirely to music, much against the wishes of his father, who foresaw for him a life of poverty. After completing his studies at the St Petersburg Conservatory, he set out for Moscow in 1866 to take up a teaching post. His financial circumstances took a turn for the better in 1877 when he acquired a wealthy patroness, Mme Nadezhda Filaretovna von Meck, who for the next fourteen years was to support him, correspond with him, but never to meet him. By 1878 he had already composed the music for the ballet *Swan Lake* and one of his most famous operas, *Eugene Onegin*. These were followed by the opera *The Queen of Spades* (1890) and the ballets *Sleeping Beauty* (1889) and *Nutcracker* (1892). Now internationally famous — in 1893 he was awarded an honorary degree by Cambridge University — he spent much of his time travelling around abroad to hear his work performed. Throughout his life, he corresponded with members of his family and his letters reveal a most delightful and generous personality. He died suddenly, under mysterious circumstances, in St Petersburg at the age of fifty-three.

Tchaikovsky was followed by his pupil Sergei Taneyev (1856-1915), who in his turn taught Sergei Rachmaninov (1873-1943), the great pianist and composer, Alexander Scriabin (1872-1915) and Reinhold Gliere (1875-1956). Another composer, Alexander Glazunov (1865-1936), was an important influence on the new generation of Russian composers during his time as a teacher and director of the St Petersburg Conservatory, before he left Russia for France in 1928.

Igor Stravinsky, born (1882) in St Petersburg, like Glazunov, was in his middle twenties when he met Sergei Diaghilev, the celebrated impresario of the Ballets Russes, and went with him to Paris. His works, particularly for the ballets *Firebird*, *Petrushka* and *Rite of Spring*, for which he is best known, owe much to the inspiration of Russian folk music. Stravinsky became a French citizen in 1934, but during the Second World War moved to the United States.

Like many other composers of the younger generation, Sergei Prokofiev (1891-1953) and Dmitry Shostakovich (1906-75) owed a debt to Glazunov: he persuaded Prokofiev's father to send him to the Conservatory to develop his musical talent, and defended the young Shostakovich's right to a scholarship there. As the latter wrote in his *Testimony*: 'This was a period of terrible famine. The gist of the scholarship was that its possessor was able to receive some groceries... If you were on the list, you lived. If you were crossed off, it was quite possible that you mighty die... The storm broke when they finally got to my name, the last one on the list. [Glazunov's] assistant suggested dropping me: "This student's name says nothing to me." And Glazunov erupted. They say he became quite wild and shouted something like: "If the name means nothing to you, then why are you sitting here with us all?"' As a result of Glazunov's protest, Shostakovich retained his scholarship and went on to produce a succession of symphonies, an opera (*Lady Macbeth of Mtsensk*), piano works and film music. In the Thirties, however, along with Prokofiev and others, he fell into disgrace for 'ideological deficiencies' and for a number of years almost all his works were banned and not performed in public. To mislead Party officials about the 'meaning' of his Fifth Symphony (first performed in 1937), Shostakovich described the work as 'joyous and optimistic'. And, as Galina Vishnevskaya relates, 'the entire pack dashed off, satisfied. The Fifth Symphony, safe from their clutches, resounded throughout the world, announcing the sufferings of great Russia.'

Prokofiev, whose most popular works are his ballet music for *Romeo and Juliet* and his Classical Symphony, came from a highly cultivated background: 'My mother loved music and my father respected it,' he wrote in his *Memoirs*. For some years after the Revolution he lived in exile, travelling on a League of Nations passport, but returned to settle with his family in Moscow in 1934. Along with other leading composers, in 1948 he was censured by the Soviet authorities for the alleged 'formalistic distortions and anti-democratic tendencies' of his music. He died in 1953 at the age of sixty-one.

Another Russian composer of the twentieth century (albeit of Armenian descent) to gain wide international popularity is Aram Khachaturian (1903-78), whose works include symphonies, ballet music and concertos for piano, violin and violoncello. During the war, Stalin decided that he and Shostakovich should collaborate on writing a new national anthem, regardless of the fact that they were composers with very different styles and methods of working. At first, neither was enthusiastic about the idea of collaboration, and after several amicable meetings, still not a note of their joint anthem had been written. Eventually, however, they managed to come up with a piece by combining Shostakovich's melody with Khachaturian's refrain. The Great Leader apparently liked it, but in the end chose a song by Grigory Alexandrov.

Ballet

Russian ballet has developed to perfection the art of dancing with the whole body, exercising it as a single expressive instrument. The strict classical training unleashes great dynamism, enabling Russian male dancers to perform the most breathtaking leaps. The prestige of Russian ballet companies also owes much to the *corps de ballet*, carefully chosen for their similar physique and trained to display absolute precision in technique. It was, in fact, a Frenchman, Marius Petipa (1819-1910), who laid the foundations of Russian dance, overseeing the development of classical ballet in Russia for the greater part of the nineteenth century. Petipa co-operated with Tchaikovsky on *The Sleeping Beauty* and *The Nutcracker*. He himself created 57 full-length ballets, 34 opera ballets and directed 17 revivals.

Ballet had first been brought to Russia in 1734 by another Frenchman, Jean Baptiste Lande. Dance schools were set up in St Petersburg and Moscow, but at that time the performers were mainly from France and Italy. The dancing master, Charles Didelot, who arrived in St Petersburg in 1801, trained Russian dancers to rival foreign ones. Almost as soon as Didelot had retired, Petipa appeared. The Imperial Ballet School of St Petersburg produced under Petipa some of its greatest ballerinas: the graceful and lyrical M. F. Kschessinska; O. I. Preobrajenska; and Anna Pavlova. After his death in 1910, the principles of classical ballet that he had taught were compiled and formulated in a treasured book, written by the dancer, Agrapina Vaganova, that became the handbook for young dancers of the Maryinsky Theatre in St Petersburg. In 1909, Russian ballet suddenly burst upon Europe, when Sergei Diaghilev, the brilliant producer, and Fokine, a leading choreographer, took a company of dancers from the Imperial School of St Petersburg to Paris. His Ballets Russes staged dazzling productions with colourful sets designed by some of Russia's finest artists, such as Benois and Bakst, but the greatest sensation were the male dancers, Nijinsky, Massine and Lifar. Nijinsky, perhaps the most famous male ballet dancer of all time, was very different from the conventional ideal, being short and sturdy in physique, but his sensationally high, floating leaps and his expressive use of his entire body excited audiences and opened up a new era in ballet.

After the Revolution, ballet maintained its technical excellence and ballet companies and schools throughout the Soviet Union enjoyed strong state support. Some outstanding new works were produced, such as Prokofiev's *Romeo and Juliet* (1946) and Khachaturian's *Spartacus* (1968), but repertories were mostly backward looking. In the Fifties, Moscow's Bolshoi Ballet and the Kirov (formerly the Imperial Ballet of St Petersburg) made their first, highly acclaimed tours in the West. The atmosphere inside the ballet schools and companies was more than usually competitive and dancers wanting to express themselves felt constrained by the restricted repertory and political pressures. In 1961 Rudolf Nureyev, Russia's greatest male dancer since Nijinsky, left the Kirov company while it was touring abroad. His example was followed by the brilliant Mikhail Baryshnikov, Natalia Makarova and others.

Today, Russian dancers are still unsurpassed in their mastery of the pure classical style, but the musical establishment can no longer rely on heavy state subsidies. Many dancers have left to join companies abroad at much higher salaries.

Film

The first film ever shown in Russia was a compilation of scenes by the Lumière brothers, screened in St Petersburg in 1896 and afterwards shown in music-halls across the country. Nicholas II was highly enthusiastic about the new invention and recorded many scenes from his family's life on film.

The Bolsheviks quickly realized the propaganda power of the moving picture and in 1919 Lenin approved the founding of the world's first university of cinematography. It was headed by leading Russian film-makers, who were to create a revolutionary film industry, sweeping away the 'salon cinematography' of the pre-Revolutionary period. The leading lights of the first generation of Russian film directors were Sergei Eisenstein, Vsevolod Pudovkin and Alexander Dovzhenko. Another remarkable pioneer was Dziga Vertov, an outstanding documentarist. Working in the era of silent film, they used poetic images and were highly innovative in their film structure. Eisenstein, for example, designed his masterpiece, *Battleship Potemkin*, in the form of a five-act classical tragedy, while Pudovkin's first feature film, *Mother*, has the form of a sonata.

Sergei Eisenstein (1898-1948) became famous at the age of twenty-seven with *Battleship Potemkin*, which so impressed the American film-makers Douglas Fairbanks and Mary Pickford that they came to Moscow to meet him and invite him to Hollywood. After making *October*, first shown in 1928, he started travelling around Europe, lecturing, and visited New York, Hollywood and Mexico. When he finally returned to Russia in 1931, the Soviet film industry was already heavily censored (through the Committee for Cinematography of the U.S.S.R.) and Eisenstein found he had earned Stalin's displeasure for staying so long abroad. In consequence, he was not allowed to make any films of his choosing for seven years, but was permitted to teach. His next film, *Bezhin Meadow*, was banned in 1935. Finally, he submitted to Stalin's will by agreeing to make a film on the subject of Alexander Nevsky. Having regained official approval through the success of this film, Eisenstein was chosen to direct another historical epic, *Ivan the Terrible*, his last film, made in 1945. Conveying a chilling atmosphere of terror and intrigue, it drew an obvious parallel between the despotic monarch and Stalin and was promptly banned. It was not shown until fifteen years after Eisenstein's death, when it was at once hailed as a masterpiece.

Propaganda films held sway during the Forties and Fifties. Motion pictures about the Great Patriotic War were released without number; the most admired is the classic *The Cranes are Flying,* a love story set in World War II, made by the Georgian film-maker, Mikhail Kalatozov, in 1957. Sergei Bondarchuk's spectacular *War and Peace* and *Waterloo* and Kozintsev's film versions of *King Lear* and *Hamlet* are also compelling watching, if sometimes a little overlong. Most admired abroad of the modern Russian directors is the innovative Andrei Tarkovsky, whose films include *Ivan's Childhood*, *Andrei Rublev*, *Solaris*, *Stalker* and *The Sacrifice*. He died in exile in 1987, almost the last of the long line of dissident artists denied freedom of expression at home.

Woodcut (lubok): girl at a distaff and peasant with a boy weaving bast shoes, first half of the eighteenth century.

MODERN
TIMES

Like people the world over, Russians want peace and prosperity, a future for their children and a secure retirement for themselves. But given the country's history, social conditions and the severe climate prevailing in most regions, life has never been easy except for a privileged few. Chekhov, whose plays are famous for their portrayal of everyday life, put the following words in the mouth of Trofimov, a character in *The Cherry Orchard*: 'We are at least two hundred years behind the times; we still have no background, no clear attitude to our past, we just philosophize, complain of depression or drink vodka.' Though these words are to some extent relevant today, the fall of the Berlin Wall in 1989 abruptly ended the long isolation of the Russian people, and a hurricane blowing in from the West swept away the old Soviet institutions and ushered in far-reaching changes, not all welcomed, in the life-style of the population.

The Russian Federation has nearly 150 million inhabitants, making it the world's sixth largest country in population after China, India, the U.S.A., Indonesia and Brazil. Besides ethnic Russians, who account for more than 80 per cent, there are more than a hundred non-Russian ethnic groups or 'nationalities'. As well as Christians (the great majority Russian Orthodox), there are many millions of Muslims, and also Jews, Buddhists and some Shamanists among the peoples of the north.

The Orthodox Church

Founded in 988, when Prince Vladimir converted from paganism, the Russian Orthodox Church is Russia's most venerable institution. The first Russian saints, canonized in 1072, were Boris and Gleb. These two murdered sons of Prince Vladimir were called 'passion bearers' because they died without resistance, in the Christian spirit. The creed of resignation is indeed one of the fundamental doctrinal elements of Orthodoxy. Moreover, in the words of the religious philosopher, Nicholas Berdyaev, the Russian 'has no philosophical justification for having temporal possessions at all, and he believes in his heart that it would be better for him to be a monk or a wandering pilgrim'.

The Soviet state was built on an atheistic pattern. Lenin, the leader of the Revolution, wrote in a letter to Gorky, dated January 1913, that there could be 'nothing more abominable than religion'. Soviet Communism had no need of God, but itself assumed a quasi-religious character: setting up its own cults and preaching the messianic role of the proletariat, the builders of a new kingdom. All the might of the new state was concentrated on eradicating 'religious superstitions' from society.

The Russian Orthodox Church had its martyrs: some 1,000 priests and 30 bishops were arrested and many of them executed between 1917 and 1921. By the end of Stalin's purges in the Thirties, only 12 Orthodox bishops remained alive. Two thirds of Moscow's ancient churches were destroyed, along with innumerable churches in other towns. Pictures of Lenin became the new icons.

Before 1917, the Russian Church was widely criticized for its servility to the state. It had lost the respect of the more educated and prosperous members of society through the drunkenness and ignorance of the clergy, and because it was seen as a tool of the autocracy. Nonetheless, its power remained great. True religious life is strengthened by persecution, for in hard times only true believers stake their lives on their faith. Many courageous priests helped the Russian Orthodox Church to survive under Communism as a Church of consolation, if not of reform.

Having discovered that he could not stamp out religion, however hard he tried, Stalin allowed the Church to function more freely during the Second World War, albeit in order to mobilize its support for the war effort. Under a scheme called the Komsomol assignment, many young Communists were meanwhile joining seminaries and training as priests in order to inform their KGB controllers of untoward activities. Three patriarchs rose by this route to the top of the church hierarchy; their identity as full-time agents of the KGB was revealed in 1992. Once again the Church was open to criticism for its compromise with the state.

Changes in religious policies were introduced in the late Eighties, making it easier for religious organizations to own their places of worship and for religious education to progress in schools. More than 1,700 churches were opened or re-opened and several monasteries were returned to the Church in the first four years of *perestroika*. This was only a fraction of its pre-Revolutionary strength of more than 50,000 churches and 1,000 monasteries, however. In the 1990s, the Church is having to come to terms with its past and confront new challenges. One problem is how to react to a rise in religious nationalism; another is how to re-establish Christian values that Communism denied.

Other Faiths

After Orthodoxy, the faith with the most adherents in Russia is Islam. Muslim communities are concentrated in Tatarstan, Bashkiria and the North Caucasus, especially Daghestan and Chechnia. The Tartars, mostly Sunni Muslims, though with an Orthodox minority, form the most numerous group. The history of Islam in Tatarstan dates back to the year 922, when the Volga Bulgar tribes, ancestors of the present-day Tatars of the region, adopted Islam and the Arabic script, some fifty years before Christianity came to Russia. By the end of the nineteenth century the growing number of Tatar-Muslim intellectuals had made Kazan the third most important centre of Islamic thought, after Cairo and Istanbul.

A resurgence of Islamic activity was evident after the fall of Communism: larger numbers began attending mosques and many new Islamic political parties were created. Communist attempts to suppress Islam were to a large degree ineffective. The Muslim faith still permeates every aspect of life in large areas of the North Caucasus: religious weddings and funerals are held and the Ramadan fast is widely observed.

The number of Jewish people living in the Russian Federation has rapidly declined since the easing of restrictions on emigration in the Eighties. From the tenth to the thirteenth century there were Slavic-speaking Jews in the state of Kievan Rus. These were subsequently assimilated by the Yiddish-speaking Ashkenazim, who moved east from Germany in the sixteenth and seventeenth centuries to escape persecution and the horrors of the Thirty Years War. In 1791 they were confined by law to the poorest western provinces, known as the Pale of Settlement. After the death of the relatively liberal tsar, Alexander II, in 1881, Jews were subjected to state-organized pogroms, particularly when difficult times called for scapegoats. Deprived of public rights, they lived in fear of the periodical massacres. Their best choice was to abjure Judaism and convert to Orthodoxy, whereupon they would be immediately treated like any other Russian. Another option was emigration: between 1898 and 1914 an estimated one and a quarter million Jews left Russia, mostly for the United States and Great Britain.

202, 203. In the post-Communist era, when demonstrations are not government orchestrated, young and old have taken to the streets, but not all for the same cause. The reforms do not enjoy universal support and are blamed by many for the disruptions, increased crime and corruption that have marred life in recent years.

204. Proof, if proof were needed, that the Russians are a hardy race. Besides playing soccer, stripped down, in the snow, they will swim in frozen rivers after breaking the ice. Toughened by the climate and not much accustomed to material comforts, they are well prepared to withstand hardships.

205. Soldiers at a station near Krasnodar
returning from the southern border of
Russia. Even with the drastic reductions
planned in the size of the armed forces,
Russia will still have by far the largest
army in Europe, and the military will
remain a potent factor in Russian affairs.

206. *What time is the train? A remote train stop near the Caspian Sea.*
The first Russian railway was built in 1837 between St Petersburg and Tsarskoye Selo, the country residence of the tsars. It was followed some six years later by the St Petersburg-Moscow line.

207. A Russian Orthodox wedding ceremony consists of two parts: the preliminary
rite of betrothal and the rite of crowning.
After the final blessing, everyone joins in
singing: 'May the couple live in joy and
peace for many years (Mnogaya leta)'.

208. This young woman with a demure,
nineteenth-century air might have stepped
out of a Chekhov play. Most Russian city
girls are very careful about their grooming
and do not like to set foot in the street without make-up and hair in place.

209. Preparing fish for lunch at the Pskov
Monastery of the Caves (Pechersky) in
northern Russia, close to the border with
Estonia (overleaf). Traditional Russian
food of the kind eaten by the common
people is not notable for its richness or
variety of ingredients. According to the old
saying: 'Cabbage broth and gruel are our
fuel.'

210. Selling eggs by the roadside avoids
the expense of travelling to the nearest
market town and paying a fee to stand in
the market. From improvised wayside
stalls, a common sight in Russia, people
sell their garden surpluses of fruit and
vegetables.

211. The cheerful stir of winter festivals helps to break the monotony of long months under snow. Sleigh-riding, cross-country skiing, ice fishing and skating are popular winter pastimes.

The Soviet state ended all restrictions on Jews and anti-Semitism was officially condemned. In the early Soviet period, they were prominent in the arts and political life and their improved position encouraged assimilation. Many adopted Russian in place of the Yiddish language. In the late Forties, however, Stalin launched an anti-Jewish campaign. Although the Jewish question has not been solved to this day, the position of practising Jews appears to have improved since the fall of Communism.

The centre of Buddhism in the Russian Federation is the Autonomous Republic of Buryatia. The Buryats, a Mongol people, adopted Buddhism in the eighteenth century from Mongolia. Before the Revolution, Buryatia had more than 40 datsans (monasteries), and 150 temples. Under Communism, Buddhists also suffered persecution for their faith: thousands of lamas were sent into exile or killed and nearly all the datsans were destroyed in Stalin's time. Now, religious buildings are being restored and Buddhist lamas practise their religion freely, openly celebrating six festivals each year.

The recent revival of Shamanism among the peoples of Siberia is a way of affirming their native traditions, their closeness to their ancestors and one another. Though the word shaman is now used loosely to mean any medicine man or magician, in origin it is a Tungus word for a member of their community with special powers of dealing with spirits. The shaman is a mystic, poet, sage, healer of the sick, guardian of the tribe and a repository of its folklore. He is believed to cure the sick by searching for their souls (since illness is thought to be caused by loss of soul), which he does by entering an ecstatic trance, accompanied by the beating of a drum. In the early 1930s, shamans were branded as practitioners of fraudulent medicine and perpetuators of outdated religious beliefs. Many were rounded up and met tragic fates, without passing on their knowledge or the secrets of their rituals. It is remarkable that there are still a few practising today and that the numbers of their followers are increasing.

The Russian Federation has emerged from under the cloak of Communism with a broad confessional pattern. Of non-Orthodox Christians, there are about half a million Catholics in the Russian Federation (considerably fewer than in the Soviet Union, since many live in the now independent Ukraine, Lithuania, Belorussia and Latvia). Protestants in the Soviet Union numbered some 247,000 Baptists, 230,000 Lutherans, 100,000 Pentecostals, and 2,200 Methodists.

Education and Health

212. A soldier's return. Like many Russians, he may be wondering what the future holds in store for himself and his family now that the Soviet Union and Communism are no more.

The Russian educational system, probably the greatest achievement of the Soviet years, has been one of the first to undergo reform. In the Soviet period, educationalists achieved an impressive 99 per cent rate of literacy and outstanding progress in general and higher education levels. The teaching of all subjects, however, was given a strong Marxist slant and was designed to educate model Soviet citizens. Since then, state schools have been given greater freedom in determining the content and methods of tuition, and students are being encouraged to adopt a more outward-looking mentality. Moreover, a large number of new private school have set up, offering a wide array of subjects (deemed unnecessary by many), ranging from Japanese to the Art of Rhetoric. The Russian system is largely based on the German one adopted at the beginning of the century and preserved by the Bolsheviks practically unchanged for seventy years.

Most children up to the age of seven can be accommodated in a preschool institution: day nursery or kindergarten. At seven the child attends primary school, and at eleven starts four years of secondary education. The young person then has a choice between staying at secondary school and applying for higher education two years later, or enrolling in a college that gives specialized vocational training. For those who elect to stay at school, admission procedures to university or a college of higher education are rigorous, entailing a medical examination, an essay on a given subject (*sochinenie*) and a number of oral examinations in three or four subjects from the curriculum, these depending on the course the student plans to take. The higher military schools (*voenniye uchilisha*) operate a similar system, with additional compulsory physical ability tests. Following recent cuts in military spending, thousands of young officers have been left with bleak prospects. The same is true of all graduates: before, employment was guaranteed by the state, but now finding a job is no longer easy.

Students are awarded grants to cover accommodation and living expenses, but although these are supposed to be inflation-linked, they are quite inadequate and students have to rely on parental support. Even so, the student population is proportionately very high. According to a 1993 survey of employed persons in St Petersburg, 56 per cent had university or college degrees. There are over 400 higher educational establishments in the Federation. The oldest universities, founded in the eighteenth century, are in Moscow (Lomonosov) and St Petersburg.

By comparison with education, the privatization of Russian medicine has hardly started. The first to defy former socialist law by going private were the dentists: even in Soviet times some dental procedures were not free of charge. Health care is still state-run with the exception of a few bold private ventures. The main problems lie in the empty Russian treasury and the disintegration of the pharmaceutical and medical supplies industries, resulting in shortages of antibiotics, vitamins and antiseptics. The medical system is structured around the polyclinics or health centres and the hospitals. Every borough in every town has a health centre (polyclinic) where patients can see a general practitioner or specialist. The polyclinic is equipped with an X-ray cabinet and its own laboratory for routine tests. However, physicians generally prefer working in hospitals, where salaries are one third higher. Medical staff are confronted by an increasing number of crime-related injuries. Alongside the usual cardiac arrests and ulcer perforations, there are ever more knife and bullet wounds to administer to in the emergency wards.

The incidence of crime has soared since the beginning of 1992, when the murder rate in Moscow was 9.6 per 100,000 people; eighteen months later its had risen to 15.5. This means the average Muscovite is ten times more likely to be 'done in' than a Londoner (although only half as likely to die an unnatural death as an inhabitant of New York). Much of the crime is related to gang warfare; the highest recorded crime rates have been in Rostov, a kind of Russian Chicago, which has established a reputation as a mafia centre.

The system of community care for the elderly inherited from the Soviet Union is poor and conditions in old people's homes are generally inadequate. The elderly are provided with only the most basic amenities: little more than a bed (but not a room) of his or her own, and a diet deficient in vegetables, fruit and vitamins. Not surprisingly, elderly people prefer staying with their families if they can, and because of the traditionally close family ties most people make every effort to care for elderly relatives, despite the cramped housing in cities.

Russia is not yet considered to be among countries facing an AIDS crisis. The number of people who are HIV positive could amount to 15,000, according to unofficial statistics — very few compared to the world-wide figure of around 13 million people with the virus. Until recently, homosexuality was illegal, carrying a penalty of five years' imprisonment.

The average life expectancy is now 65.8 years, no higher than in some developing countries such as Algeria and Syria. For men, it has plunged to 59 years, the lowest level since the 1960s, while women live on average 73 years. Throughout Russia there has been a rise in cardiovascular diseases among men, breast and uterine cancer among women, and lung cancer for both groups. Smoking is still far more widespread in Russia than in the West (although cigarette prices have rocketed with inflation). Soviet medicine successfully eliminated polio, many children's infections and malaria, and the incidence of tuberculosis was much reduced, but it seems that the number of poverty-related diseases is increasing and the general health of the population has declined. This can be attributed to poor diet in consequence of growing financial hardship, and the rise of water and air pollution: over 40 per cent of illnesses in the Russian Federation are thought to be connected with the environment.

The Family and Home

Many Russians turn for support to their family. It is common for three generations to live together, though the size of the family is shrinking in most parts of the country. There has been a steady fall in the birth rate: the average number of children is now two. Though children are doted on and indulged, parents feel obliged to limit the size of their families, mainly for financial reasons and because of inadequate housing. Birth control is in a dismal state, with abortion the most popular method. Most women have several abortions — six or seven is said to be the average. The number of abortions in the former Soviet Union, according to official statistics, was around 6.5 million annually, while only 5.6 million children were born. The majority of the population tolerates abortion, in spite of its spiritual implications. The views of the Russian Orthodox Church on the subject have yet to be expressed.

Marriage is a civil contract, though the ceremony taking place at the Palace of Marriages is a solemn, public occasion. The state permits religious and other traditional wedding ceremonies and these are are becoming more popular throughout the country. In the big cities especially, the divorce rate is very high, with alcoholism and adultery two of the main causes. Another is lack of privacy through flat-sharing.

In 1993 rent was on average less than one tenth of an average monthly wage. Since 1989 many flats have become privately owned, their long-term occupants having been allowed to buy them for a symbolic price. Buying a new flat is much more expensive and far beyond the reach of most people. The majority of families in towns live in small two- or three-room apartments in purpose-built blocks of flats in varying states of repair. New house-owners have to face maintenance costs that were formerly paid for by the local authorities. However, low-cost water and electricity supplies are still subsidized by the state.

It would not be an exaggeration to say that the average Russian woman is one of the most highly qualified in the world. According to statistics, women make up 82 per cent of teachers, including two thirds of staff in high schools, 51 per cent of doctors, and more than half of students in higher education. Many more women become scientists, engineers and technicians than in the West. However, their representation in government, the higher echelons of the administration and upper management is proportionately small, the men remaining in charge of the female work force. Russia boasts the world's highest level of female employment: 92 per cent according to a survey published at the end of 1992. There is no conception of the weaker sex here: they work in heavy industry, on building sites and sweeping the streets.

Almost every woman is expected to be both a housewife and a bread-winner, for apart from minor household repairs, the typical Russian husband plays a fairly minor part in domestic affairs. Housework requires considerable physical strength since most of it is done by hand. Although appliances like washing machines are now available in the shops, most people cannot afford them. Another tiring and time-consuming part of the daily round is shopping, involving endless searching for goods and standing in line. Those with enough money, preferably foreign currency, can supply themselves with fresh foodstuffs at the peasant markets. Most men do help their wives on their plot of land, if they have one, growing and picking an abundance of summer fruit, as well as vegetables, to augment the meagre supplies in the shops. Women have to work extra hard in the summer preparing fruit preserves (*vareniye*) and pickles.

Excessive consumption of intoxicating beverages is widespread in Russia, and the cause of many family problems and economic ills. Attempts to curb this by raising the price or rationing supplies have so far proved ineffective. The average adult drinks an estimated 10 or 12 litres of pure alcohol a year — equivalent to a bottle of vodka a week. Hard drinking is blamed for delinquency, road accidents, accidents and absenteeism at work, and over half of divorces. This is not, of course, a new problem. Alcohol has always provided a temporary escape from the long dark winters, harsh climate and grinding poverty endured by most Russians for centuries. For the aristocracy, it relieved the boredom of life on their estates.

Of the traditional alcoholic drinks, the mildest is *kvas*, made from fermented rye bread and tasting not unlike ginger beer. The strongest is vodka, made by distilling grain and repeatedly purifying it to increase its alcoholic strength and refine its flavour. In the past the government controlled all supplies, guaranteeing the quality, but today the old system has broken down and there is no knowing what goes into some vodkas.

Sport and Leisure

Sport, both as a form of healthy mass recreation and as a means to boost international prestige, received a large measure of official encouragement and financial support in the Soviet Union. Young people were talent-spotted and intensively groomed for international stardom in almost every type of sport, from athletics and gymnastics to ice-skating and swimming. In the special schools and sports clubs, the selected talents were subjected to long hours of gruelling training, but since success at sport was a passport to privileges such as foreign travel, there was no shortage of eager candidates. The incentives are still powerful in the post-Soviet era, when sportsmen and women who make their mark in international competition can count on earning high financial rewards abroad.

Even though the Soviet pool of talent has been split up among the independent CIS states, Russia is still a sporting superpower. Among the most popular team games are soccer, basketball and volleyball, with soccer attracting the biggest crowds. Not surprisingly, given the climate, Russians excel at winter sports, particularly ice-hockey, Nordic ski-ing and skating.

Chess is another popular pastime: there are innumerable chess clubs throughout the country and people can often be seen in fine weather playing in parks, with a crowd of interested observers standing round. Promising young players apply to the state for a grant, and if they make the grade, receive financial support to do nothing else but study and play chess. In return they are obliged to teach chess to younger players and to represent their country around the world. For years Russians have dominated world team and individual championships.

For health reasons or else just to chat with friends, some Russians regularly go to the *banya* or public bath-house, enjoying a hot bath, sweating in the steam room, or using bundles of birch twigs for an invigorating 'massage'. Traditional bath-houses, usually in the form of an oblong log cabin, are still built in rural areas in northern Russia. Most city and town dwellers have baths and showers in their apartments and so visiting the *banya* is not obligatory.

The disintegration of the Soviet Union has turned holiday making into a problem for millions of Russians, used to cheap and easy travel within the country and in the former satellite states. The Black Sea coast remains the most popular holiday area, despite the dispute between Russia and Ukraine. Since the Department of Railways disintegrated, leaving no successor capable of coping efficiently with the huge railway network, train services have become unreliable. But no obstacle is big enough to deter Russian holidaymakers craving a glimpse of the southern sun. Rail travel is, moreover, still cheaper than flying, since Aeroflot is continually putting up fares to cope with rising inflation. Many Russians are travelling to western Europe for the first time following the easing of travel restrictions.

Looking Ahead

Not surprisingly, most Russians are flabbergasted by the revolutionary events of recent years. How to cope with inflation, how to save something from their meagre earnings and pay bills? These are new headaches for millions of citizens. Adapting to the new life-style is not easy. Pensioners and the unemployed are the most vulnerable groups. Indexing of pensions has been introduced, but many elderly people have lost all their life savings in the surges of inflation. Moreover, growing material inequality is raising racial and national tensions. While the attitude of the average Russian towards foreigners is usually welcoming and hospitable, there is a tendency to blame the non-Russian ethnic groups for many of the country's woes, and a degree of xenophobia explains, in part, the rise of Russian nationalism. Attitudes of distrust of the West cultivated over decades by the Soviet media cannot be changed overnight.

A revolution is in progress in Russia as the world looks on with bated breath, speculating as to what course the country will follow. The grandchildren of those who survived the Revolution of 1917 will tell their grandchildren how they lived through *perestroika* and the collapse of the Soviet Union. What the eventual outcome of this restructuring will be depends primarily on the Russian people, who have survived so many upheavals, wars and other disasters in the past, but the support and encouragement of the more prosperous members of the international community is vital in ensuring that Russia moves in a direction that will bring benefits to itself and the world at large.

CHRONOLOGY

800 B.C.	Slavs living on the territory of present-day European Russia
600-300 B.C.	Scythians and Greek colonies in southern Russia
200 B.C.-200 A.D.	Sarmatians control much of central Russia and Romans the Black Sea region
200-400 A.D.	Goths dominant from the Don to Carpathians
450	Hunnish Empire from the Volga to Danube
560-600	Avar khanate stretches from the Elbe to Don
650-750	Khazar kaganate rules eastern European Russia
880	Kievan Rus ruled by the Varangians (Vikings); Oleg, son of Rurik, makes Kiev his capital
889	Prince Vladimir and his subjects converted to Christianity
1054	Death of Prince Yaroslav, followed eventually by the break-up of Kievan Rus into 12 principalities
1136-1478	Novgorod a fully independent republic
1219-1241	Mongol conquest of all Russia except Novgorod
1261	Muscovy begins to dominate other principalities
1380	Prince Dimitry Donskoy defeats Mongols at Kulikovo.
1462-1505	Reign of Prince Ivan III the Great; Muscovy thows off Mongol yoke and rapidly expands
1547	Ivan IV the Terrible crowned 'Tsar of all the Russias'
1552-56	Ivan IV conquers khanates of Kazan and Astrakhan
1578	Novgorod razed, its inhabitants massacred
1584-1598	Reign of Fedor I; his death ends the Rurikid dynasty
1598-1613	'Time of Troubles'; invasions by Poles and Swedes
1613	Michael Romanov crowned tsar
1654	Unification of Russia and Ukraine
1670-1	Rebellion led by Don Cossack Stenka Razin
1682-1725	Reign of Peter I the Great
1703	St Petersburg founded, and made the capital in 1712
1709	Swedes defeated at Poltava
1721	Treaty of Nystadt ends Great Northern War; Russia gains Baltic states
1725-1730	Reign of Catherine I, Peter's widow
1730-1740	Reign of Empress Anna
1740-1761	Reign of Empress Elizabeth
1762-1796	Reign of Catherine II the Great; expansion of Russian Empire eastward and westward
1773-5	Peasant and Cossack rebellion led by Emelyan Pugachev
1796-1801	Reign of Paul
1801-25	Reign of Alexander I
1812	French invasion of Russia, followed by Russian occupation of Paris
1817-62	Caucasian wars
1825-55	Reign of Nicholas I, which starts with the Decembrist uprising
1853-6	Crimean War
1855-81	Reign of Alexander II, the 'Tsar Liberator'
1861	Emancipation of serfs
1874	Compulsory military service introduced
1881	Assassination of Alexander II
1881-94	Reign of Alexander III
1894-1917	Reign of Nicholas II, last of the Romanov tsars
1905	Bloody Sunday in St Petersburg followed by October Manifesto promising civil liberties

1914	Russia enters the First World War
1917	March, Nicholas abdicates; Provisional Government takes over October, Bolsheviks led by V.I. Lenin seize power
1918-1921	Civil War
1924	Death of Lenin, J.V. Stalin takes over power
1928-32	Collectivization of agriculture
1939	Soviet-German Pact
1941	Germany attacks the Soviet Union
1942-3	Battle of Stalingrad
1945	Red Army enters Berlin, Germany capitulates
1953	Death of Stalin; N.S. Kruschchev eventually assumes leadership
1964	Khrushchev ousted by L.I. Brezhnev
1982	Death of Brezhnev, succeeded in turn by Y.A. Andropov and K.U. Chernenko
1985	M.S. Gorbachev takes over leadership after Chernenko's death, inaugurates reforms
1991	Boris Yeltsin elected president of the Russian Federation
1991	Dissolution of the U.S.S.R., formation of the Commonwealth of Independent States

Diamond crown of Peter the Great, engraving.

INDEX